Welcome to Thebes

by
Moira Buffini

SERVING THEATRE

SINCE 1830

WWW.SAMUELFRENCH.CO.UK
WWW.SAMUELFRENCH.COM

Welcome to Thebes was first performed in the Olivier auditorium of the National Theatre, London, on 15 June 2010. The cast was as follows:

THEBANS

Megaera **Madeline Appiah**
Sergeant Miletus **Michael WIldman**
Junior Lieutenant Scud **Omar Brown or René Gray**

Eurydice **Nikki Amuka-Bird**

Prince Tydeus **Chuk Iwuji**
Pargeia **Rakie Ayola**

Haemon **Simon Manyonda**
Antigone **Vinette Robinson**
Ismene **Tracy Ifeachor**

Tiresias **Bruce Myers**
Harmonia **Alexia Khadime**
Ploykleitos **Daniel Poyser**

Aglaea **Aicha Kossoko**
Thalia **Joy Richardson**
Euphrosyne **Pamela Nomvete**

Eunomia **Zara Tempest-Walters**
Bia **Karlina Grace**
Helia **Clare Perkins**
Eris **Irma Inniss**
Xenophanes **Cornelius Macarthy**

ATHENIANS

Theseus **David Harewood**
Phaeax **Ferdinand Kingsley**
Talthybia **Jacqueline Defferary**
Enyalius **Victor Power**
Plautus **Daniel Fine**
Ichnaea **Jessie Burton**

Director **Richard Eyre**
Designer **Tim Hatley**
Lighting Designer **Neil Austin**
Music **Stephen Warbeck**
Choreographer **Scarlett Mackmin**
Sound Designer **Rich Walsh**

Author's Note

I've been asked to write an author's note
To explain why I don't put all the full stops in.
The text is not poetry
It is drama
It needs to be useful to actors
And I think this is

Other plays by Moira Buffini published by Samuel French Ltd

Loveplay
A Vampire Story

Moira Buffini's plays include *Blavatsky's Tower* (Machine Room), *Gabriel* (Soho Theatre), *Silence* (Birmingham Rep), *Loveplay* (Royal Shakespeare Company), *Dinner* (National Theatre and West End), *Dying for It*, adapted from *The Suicide* by Nikolai Erdman (Almeida), *A Vampire Story* (NT Connections), *Marianne Dreams* (Almeida), *Welcome to Thebes* (National Theatre), *Handbagged* (Tricycle Theatre) and *wonder.land*, created with Damon Albarn and Rufus Norris (National Theatre).

CHARACTERS

MEGAERA, *a female soldier*
SERGEANT MILETUS
JUNIOR LIEUTENANT SCUD
EURYDICE, *president of Thebes*
HAEMON, *her son*
ANTIGONE, *her niece*
ISMENE, *her niece*

THESEUS, *first citizen of Athens*
PHAEAX, *his aide*
TALTHYBIA, *a diplomat*

TIRESIAS, *a seer*
HARMONIA, *his guide*
POLYKLEITOS, *a mechanic*
PRINCE TYDEUS, *leader of the opposition*
PARGEIA, *a senator*
AGLAEA, *Foreign Secretary*
THALIA, *Minister of Justice*
EUPHROSYNE, *Minister of Finance*

EUNOMIA, *a student of law*
BIA, *Minister of Trade and Industry*
HELIA, *Minister of Agriculture*

ERIS, *Chief of police*
XENOPHANES, *Minister of Education*
ENYALIUS, *head of Athenian security*
PLAUTUS, *Athenian security*
ICHNAEA, *Athenian secret services*

Aides, bodyguards, attendants, citizens.

SETTING

A city named Thebes,
Somewhere in the twenty-first century.

PROLOGUE

Boom

Three Theban soldiers enter: **MEGAERA**, *a woman of twenty,* **MILETUS** *a* **SERGEANT** *of maybe thirty,* **JUNIOR LIEUTENANT** **SCUD**, *a boy of thirteen. They come through the auditorium.*

MEGAERA OK shut up

MILETUS Anyone still talking now shut up

SCUD SILENCE

MEGAERA Nobody make any sudden moves, nobody get up

MILETUS Stay in your seats

SCUD PHONES

MILETUS Phones – any fucking disco tunes and I will not answer for my men

SCUD You check them NOW

MEGAERA Put the booklets down. Don't read that shit

SCUD All of you make sure those fuckers don't go off

MILETUS Listen to the Junior Lieutenant – he don't like mobile phones

SCUD They have bad energy and they affect your brain. I'm telling you for your own good

MEGAERA Anyone who wants the toilet I don't care. You missed your chance

By now all three are on the stage. It is dawn.

SCUD You've got to look for bomblets

1

MILETUS I am insulted if the truth be known

SCUD Get looking

MILETUS Our orders are to search for unexploded sub-munitions. No equipment. For our mine detector we have got the Junior Lieutenant here

SCUD They are called bomblets – and they're yellow.

Look like little cans of fizz

And children pull on them because their thirst is bad

BOOM

And you become a rain of meat

And women pulling bits of you from out their hair

And screaming oh disgusting get me some shampoo

MILETUS What are you doing?

MEGAERA I'm sitting down here on my arse

MILETUS Why?

MEGAERA I haven't finished with these people

MILETUS What d'you want with them?

SCUD jumps on some rubble.

SCUD BOOM

MEGAERA To welcome them to Thebes

MILETUS Don't tell them all your shit

MEGAERA Why not?

MILETUS They'll leave

MEGAERA Are you the expert?

MILETUS I would leave

MEGAERA I'm going to tell them Theban politics

MILETUS No one understands that

SCUD jumps on another pile of rubble.

SCUD BOOM

MILETUS Easy son

Be easy

You stay right by my side

MILETUS *moves away, with* **SCUD**. **MEGAERA** *holds up her gun.*

MEGAERA The only politics in Thebes is this.

This has been the government for years.

I don't know how it started; I don't care

Some brother fighting brother for the power.

My politics began the day the soldiers came.

This is my shit and if you're scared to hear it

Close your eyes.

We heard their guns and ran.

I could feel bullets wooshing past my face.

I saw a man turn round and try to stop one with his hand

Because he thought 'what's this?'

As if the bullet was a fly.

Woosh

They trapped us by the river.

If I could describe you how it felt

The way they held me down and tore

You would be sick I know you would

Or scream and we'd be here all day

While you had counselling and cried.

After five or six I was unconscious I suppose.

The soldiers must have thought that I was dead

Because when I came to, I found myself

In a pile of bodies. My mother

And my sisters seethed with ants.

This is your introduction to our state

'Cause everybody has a tale like this.

I slipped into the river, floated to the fields.

Time was not even. It was odd.

It bends and it's misshapen in my mind.

A day was like a month, a month a year.

I don't think that I spoke one word.

I ate forest nuts and beetles poor old me

My monthly bleeding never came again.

SCUD BOOM

MEGAERA And then Miletus found me

He's the sergeant there, my brother now.

He put this gun into my hand and

Made me human once again.

When we fall upon our enemies

– Always the men who did that to me –

Feelings come on me like I don't know

I am not scared of anything

No pain about my family

No cares

I am all powerful, all fire

I am revenge, Megaera; I am fury

Woosh.

The furies have no laws other than their own

Which even Zeus himself has to obey.

These are my laws now

And this, my life of politics.

Peace?

Never, not for me

MILETUS Megaera

SCUD Dead bloke

> **MILETUS** *and* **SCUD** *have discovered a corpse.* **MEGAERA** *approaches.*

MILETUS Look at that uniform

New boots, the golden braid

SCUD *spins, startled. He raises his rifle.*

SCUD Felt fingers down my back

MEGAERA Well they ain't his

He's maggot food

MILETUS This is Polynices

MEGAERA How do you know?

MILETUS His necklace

MEGAERA Fuck

MILETUS General Polynices

SCUD Did we fight for him?

MEGAERA *spits.*

MILETUS No. He's the one who pulled you out of school; his men

SCUD *reacts to this, the memory like a cuff.*

When I picked you up I was with Creon's men, remember? We fought for him til the stupid fucker got dismembered. Then for Adrastus till he set himself on fire. Then we were in the forest fighting everyone. Last we joined Eteocles. He's the one who still had food

SCUD Who do we fight for now?

MEGAERA That is the question, Scud

SCUD I fought for you

MILETUS I know

SCUD The ghosts are grey

MILETUS Come on

MILETUS *leaves with* **SCUD**.

MEGAERA Welcome

Welcome to Thebes

ACT ONE

Scene One
Arriving

Enter TIRESIAS *led by a* HARMONIA, *a girl.*

Enter POLYKLEITOS, *a mechanic. He sits amid a pile of rifle parts, dismantling weapons.*

Enter ANTIGONE, *barefoot, objectless, alone.*

The sound of a helicopter approaching from afar.

Enter Thebans and Athenians, preparing for a state event.

ANTIGONE *watches them as if their actions make no sense.*

TALTHYBIA *runs on; an Athenian aide. Bottled water, paperwork, bad choice of footwear.*

HARMONIA *is begging.* TALTHYBIA *declines to give her a coin and exits hurriedly.*

HARMONIA *approaches* ANTIGONE.

ANTIGONE I have nothing

Nothing no

TIRESIAS You have not survived this war, Antigone

You're breathing but you're not alive.

ANTIGONE *begins to walk away. His voice arrests her.*

The dead see everything you do

In darkness they have eyes that never close

6

Up here, everyone is blind

Think hard where you belong

ANTIGONE Don't talk to me, Tiresias

TIRESIAS You and your sister

Last remnants of a cursed house

Follow your destiny, Antigone

The helicopter, louder. **ANTIGONE** *exits.*

TALTHYBIA *enters. A makeshift Theban choir begin to sing a national anthem.*

Other Athenian men and women enter in silk and linen suits; Theban officials in cheaper suits or trying to hold together their national dress in the face of the helicopter's gale.

The helicopter becomes deafening. One of the choir runs. **HARMONIA** *seeks cover.*

TIRESIAS *remains, the only still point in the scene.*

Helicopters are obviously beasts of terror in Thebes, for the makeshift choir has fled.

TALTHYBIA *loses her hairdo. Everyone crouches in the blast.*

The blast dies down. **TALTHYBIA** *rushes off, followed by soldiers and aides.*

Bodyguards and aides cross with all the luggage and paraphernalia of a diplomatic stay. **HARMONIA** *stands up, trying to see.*

THESEUS *enters, a confident man in his prime.* **TALTHYBIA** *is at his side.*

TALTHYBIA Theseus, I am Talthybia

It's such a / pleasure

THESEUS Thebes

TALTHYBIA We have our people working on a new hotel and embassy but at the moment there's two options, sir; the compound where our military are or there's an invitation from the president elect, Eurydice, to stay here at the presidential palace. We've checked it over; basic but OK. A lot of art and artefacts; no electricity. There is no national grid right now

THESEUS I'm staying here?

TALTHYBIA It's a building of historic interest and much cooler than the compound. It also gets the breeze; built by Cadmus and Harmonia who founded Thebes

THESEUS Do they have internet?

TALTHYBIA At the compound we have internet

THESEUS They got a phone?

TALTHYBIA Mobiles, yes amazingly. They seem to go on working even when the power is down

THESEUS I want to call my wife

TALTHYBIA I'm sure they're setting up a private line

THESEUS Right now

I feel like telling her I'm here

TALTHYBIA Please borrow mine sir. It would be such a privilege –

THESEUS Sure

TALTHYBIA To know that I've assisted with your personal communication

PHAEAX *joins them.* THESEUS *dials.*

Everyone has mobiles; it's astonishing. You go out to the villages and even in these little one-goat towns without a single flushing loo, everyone is talking on a mobile phone

PHAEAX *(to* TALTHYBIA*)* Excuse me where's the band?

TALTHYBIA Yes actually, there is no band

THESEUS Hey Phaedra – guess where I am

Oh – could you get her?

PHAEAX Theseus was told there'd be a band. He is expecting one

TALTHYBIA Well very / sorry but

PHAEAX If there wasn't one I should have been informed

TALTHYBIA I did my best to get a band. The Thebans / told me
this

PHAEAX He likes the music here

TALTHYBIA The band are dead except the bass guitar

He's alive but only one hand left

THESEUS / She what?

TALTHYBIA So then I tried to organise a choral group;

Authentic local sound

THESEUS / OK

TALTHYBIA But people don't like helicopters here. They've gone

PHAEAX Would you explain that to him please?

Because this is insulting

I can't even see a fucking flag

PHAEAX exits.

THESEUS Get her to call me on this number; thanks

TALTHYBIA The city's still unstable, sir

We didn't think it wise to make a lot of fuss

THESEUS Quite so. I'd better keep this phone; she's going to call
me back

TALTHYBIA That's absolutely

What an honour

Sir, I did intend for there to be some music as a welcome but –

THESEUS No commotion. Good

TALTHYBIA I'm glad you think so

THESEUS Yes. I've come here in humility

I want to see first-hand what we Athenians have done

We've given common people here control of their own fate

The gift of democratic government

TALTHYBIA The voting; frankly it was moving –

THESEUS They need to see what democratic leadership can be

PHAEAX *re-enters.*

PHAEAX Sir, they have some rooms prepared. Perhaps you'd like to freshen up? Before you meet the president elect

THESEUS Just look at this old palace

TALTHYBIA Soon to be renamed the congress

THESEUS Dionysus; he was born here

The great god Frenzy

PHAEAX Yes sir

THESEUS Bacchus

Pulled from the thigh of Zeus

Maybe right where we stand

PHAEAX Forgive me sir that's not correct

He wasn't pulled from the thigh here

He was sewn into it.

/ Zeus gestated the foetal god –

THESEUS Dionysus comes from Thebes

That's what I'm saying

PHAEAX Yes sir

THESEUS Have they got plumbing here?

TALTHYBIA We've been installing it. No hot water but

THESEUS I like my water cold.

So this is Thebes

You can almost smell the history

EURYDICE *is dressing.* **ISMENE** *attends her.*

SCENE TWO
Dressing

EURYDICE First, I will express my disbelief

ISMENE In what?

EURYDICE Disbelief they voted for us
  I can't believe it

ISMENE Well they did

EURYDICE I only fought because there had to be an opposition
  We could not let the violence go on
  Could not have another Polynices
  So I found myself –
  It's literally like that
  Found myself with others
  Acting to oppose
  Speaking
  Words issuing from out my mouth
  In torrents
  A solace from the pain
  I never dreamt that politics would be my path
  I've always hated them
  Hated standing there at Creon's side
  Watching the ebb and flow of power from man to man
  The little games of consequence
  Experiments with human lives.
  Politics is what I've always fought against.
  But now I've won
  I'm feeling sick
  I've promised them pipe dreams, Ismene

ISMENE You've promised peace

EURYDICE I'm feeling I might actually throw up

ISMENE Well if you do, please miss the outfit

EURYDICE Creon had principles until he was in power.

I saw what power did to him.

I watched the man diminish as it took its hold.

I watched his hopes and values all corrode

ISMENE The people know you're different

EURYDICE Am I, though?

Am I?

What will it do to me?

Ismene

ISMENE Yes

EURYDICE I'm meeting Theseus

ISMENE I know; it's so exciting

EURYDICE I look awful in this dress

ISMENE I haven't finished yet

You need accessories

A scarf, you see?

Connotations of humility

But powerful mystique.

It softens all your lines

And then the architecture works

EURYDICE Oh yes

ISMENE You need an elegant but manly watch

To show that Time is your new god

EURYDICE I love you

ISMENE What about a bag?

EURYDICE No bag

ISMENE Athenians all have them

This one is designer

EURYDICE I'm walking out into a world of men

Unadorned and empty-handed

ISMENE *holds her.*

ISMENE Bring us justice

AGLAEA *enters.*

AGLAEA He is here

EURYDICE I'm ready

AGLAEA You have made a terrible mistake

EURYDICE Don't you like it?

AGLAEA You have not invited Sparta

EURYDICE Oh

AGLAEA I assumed you'd have the sense to see they must be here

EURYDICE If I invite the Spartans, Theseus might leave. I'll not antagonise him

AGLAEA We need Sparta or he'll walk all over you. We need a bidding war with Thebes as the prize –

EURYDICE Athens stands for everything we've fought for; freedom and democracy –

AGLAEA For their own citizens

EURYDICE Sparta is secretive, oppressive and aggressive

They want an empire here by stealth –

AGLAEA So does Theseus

We are staring at the Titans

Monsters both –

Both poised to scavenge us

Be practical

We have to play them

One against the other

EURYDICE That's a dangerous game for novices

AGLAEA It's the only way we stand to win

We need money, not ideals

Stability will only come with economic growth

EURYDICE I will not get into bed with a regime

That uses fear and violence to control.

In Athens human rights are shrined in law

AGLAEA They are a luxury

When we have food enough / and sanitation

EURYDICE Our principles won us this election

And in the ruins of this shattered state

They are the only shreds of dignity we have.

I put my trust in Theseus – on principle

AGLAEA Then go and kiss his hairy hand

EURYDICE I'm sorry that we disagree

AGLAEA Nice dress

She starts to go.

Be careful please

I know he wears a splendid suit

Sewn with a democratic thread;

He's still a warlord with a warlord's heart

EURYDICE All men are not so

AGLAEA He fights his wars behind a desk

But don't imagine that the beast is tame

EUPHROSYNE Eurydice, they've found a body by the walls. It is the corpse of Polynices

EURYDICE *and* **ISMENE** *are profoundly affected.*

EURYDICE How do you know?

EUPHROSYNE His necklace

EURYDICE I must see him

EUPHROSYNE Come child

AGLAEA Don't keep Theseus waiting

EURYDICE *(going)* Nothing takes precedence

> **EURYDICE** *and* **EUPHROSYNE** *exit.*

AGLAEA Is this the way it goes?

> Already she has put her own needs first

ISMENE Polynices killed her son

AGLAEA I know

ISMENE My cousin Menoceus. He was only just thirteen

AGLAEA I know

ISMENE Polynices pulled the brains from out his skull while still he
lived –

AGLAEA Yes Ismene, yes

> But it is past.

> Her job is to secure our future

ISMENE Why don't you go and meet him?

AGLAEA Because I am incapable of hiding what I think

> And I think Theseus a bag of wind

> **THESEUS** *with* **TALTHYBIA** *and* **PHAEAX.**

SCENE THREE
Predicting

THESEUS So on a scale of one to ten, exactly how fucked is this place?

TALTHYBIA I'd say it's been up to eleven.

Thebes is conflict-devastated

THESEUS Currently around?

TALTHYBIA Eight or nine

Still very volatile

THESEUS OK

TALTHYBIA The election has improved things but there is no infrastructure whatsoever; thousands of displaced, traumatised people, destruction of homes, agriculture, industry. The violence was bestial. There were seven different armed militias all advancing on the city

THESEUS I heard they ate each other

TALTHYBIA Yes, combatants used to eat the brains of those they killed in order to inherit strength and skill. Apparently a custom from pre-Cadmus times. There has been indescribable brutality. I put accounts into my briefing

THESEUS You wrote that briefing?

TALTHYBIA Yes sir

THESEUS What's your name again?

TALTHYBIA Talthybia

THESEUS That's right. Nice piece of work, Talthybia

TALTHYBIA Thank you

THESEUS It almost put me off my in-flight meal

TALTHYBIA May I say on behalf of everybody working on the ground, how very glad we are to see you. Your visit's a terrific boost to our morale

THESEUS They have democracy and now they can rise out of this disgusting quagmire

TALTHYBIA That is our hope

THESEUS So – we have a conference tomorrow

TALTHYBIA Yes indeed

THESEUS And when do we begin to pull our peacekeepers out?

PHAEAX In ten days time

TALTHYBIA But sir –

PHAEAX Where is the president elect? She should be here by now

> ELSEWHERE: **EURYDICE** *is staring at Polynices's corpse.* **EUPHROSYNE** *and the soldiers accompany. She cannot tear her eyes away.*

TALTHYBIA It's probably some urgent matter

PHAEAX She can have no conception of your status, sir

EUPHROSYNE What shall we do with him?

TALTHYBIA It's my belief that Thebes will need our presence here long-term. There's a tremendous will for change but it won't happen overnight. In Eurydice, the people have chosen a leader / who –

THESEUS Who is not here

EURYDICE Do nothing

Let me think

PHAEAX This is clearly someone sir, with no experience

TALTHYBIA She has experienced a decade of extreme and bloody war. When Creon died, the generals put her under house arrest. And even from her prison here she fought. She gave her strength to this amazing movement of women all risking their lives for peace

THESEUS The women, right

TALTHYBIA They would congregate in numbers and place themselves in the line of fire. During the peace talks they barricaded all the men inside the building, shamed them into peace. I find it deeply moving, inspirational

THESEUS Yes / quite so

TALTHYBIA She's given people hope

EURYDICE Polynices

TALTHYBIA The leaders of this grass-roots movement; they are now the government

ELSEWHERE: **EURYDICE** *and* **EUPHROSYNE** *exit.*

PHAEAX The minister of finance was a teacher in a rural school

TALTHYBIA Yes; she's incorruptible

She's sweeping out the toads, the ghosts, the layabouts

She'll spend our money on the people not on palaces and cars

THESEUS There's no such thing as incorruptible

TALTHYBIA Eurydice has said that everything must change.

The men have shown what they can do for Thebes

And now the women will

PHAEAX Woah

THESEUS But what do we think; do we trust her?

TALTHYBIA Yes I think / she's –

THESEUS Do we like her?

TALTHYBIA – very good news

THESEUS Because she isn't here. Why is that?

TIRESIAS Welcome blind traveller

THESEUS I'm sorry?

TIRESIAS *is with* **HARMONIA**. *She holds out a hand for money.*

PHAEAX What's this person doing here?

TIRESIAS Welcome to the country of the blind

PHAEAX I thought we had secured this area

TALTHYBIA He's a beggar. That's his place. We've checked him and he's not a threat. Don't look so scared; you don't have to give him anything

THESEUS I don't have any Theban currency

TALTHYBIA The begging's kind of overwhelming. It simply isn't possible to carry that much change – so I've developed strategies. I only give to grandmothers; they're the poorest and most selfless. Sometimes I give to exceptionally hideous amputees but

THESEUS That is a grandmother

TALTHYBIA No sir, excuse me; that's a man

THESEUS It's a woman

TIRESIAS Give me your hand King Theseus

THESEUS Actually my title is First Citizen. We don't have kings in Athens; we're a democratic state

TIRESIAS The future holds my clear unblinking gaze

It's only in the present that I'm blind.

Why don't you let me tell you what I see?

THESEUS Female, unquestionably

TALTHYBIA Male

TIRESIAS I'm both.

I saw two serpents mating on a path

TALTHYBIA We have no interest, sorry

TIRESIAS *(taking* **THESEUS***' hand)* Intertwined

Encoiled, jaws wrapped round each other

Poison dripping in mistrust even as

They slithered propagation

THESEUS Oh OK

TIRESIAS The sight disgusted me. It seemed too human.

I tore the slippery beasts apart

And crushed one with my heel. It was the she.

As punishment the snakes made me a woman

THESEUS The snakes changed you into a woman?

TIRESIAS No punishment, say I, to be a female.

Lying back, my legs spread wide, I know

Ten times the bliss I suffered as a man.

We suffer pleasure as we suffer pain

You know this to be true. So does your wife

THESEUS My wife?

TIRESIAS She's young; you married her last year

THESEUS Good guess

TIRESIAS She harbours love for someone else.

She doesn't want to but it's there, a love.

It grows in her like cancer day by day.

It will consume her

THESEUS *pulls back his hand, deeply affected.*

THESEUS What the fuck

TALTHYBIA He's just a bullshit beggar, sir

HARMONIA *holds out her hand for money.*

Move along now please. You get him out of here

EURYDICE *enters with* **EUPHROSYNE**.

THESEUS I want internet, hot water. I don't care if you drag the generator up the hill yourself. I want a private line, Phaedra on the end of it. And where's the fucking president elect? I've flown all the way from Athens to witness her inauguration and she doesn't have the decency to meet me

EURYDICE Theseus

Hello

EURYDICE *takes his hand.*

Welcome to Thebes

THESEUS Eurydice

EURYDICE We're thrilled to see you

Thank you so much for coming.

It means a great deal to Thebes and to me

THESEUS Congratulations on your victory

EURYDICE Thank you. My late husband Creon was a great admirer
of all things Athenian. So am I, especially democracy

THESEUS That's good to hear

You look smaller than your photograph

EURYDICE So do you

Let me walk you round our gardens. Miraculously they survived
the war – and they're so cool at this time of the day. Do you
have humming birds in Athens?

They exit, followed by the aides, bodyguards. **TALTHYBIA** *gives*
HARMONIA *some money.*

TALTHYBIA *(to* **TIRESIAS***)* So what about me? Will you tell me my
life?

TIRESIAS I cannot see you

TALTHYBIA I'm here. What's my destiny, old man?

TIRESIAS You are a faceless nameless minion. You don't have one

HAEMON, EUNOMIA *and Senator* **THALIA** *enter.* **HAEMON** *'s*
eyes have suffered serious injury. The approach **POLYKLEITOS,**
a mechanic.

Scene Four
Losing

THALIA My name is Thalia, I'm a senator of your new government.
We're here collecting testimony

POLYKLEITOS So I've heard

THALIA Would you like to contribute?

POLYKLEITOS Why would I?

THALIA It's so important that we speak
That we are heard

POLYKLEITOS You are evangelists, I think

HAEMON Evangelists for truth and reconciliation

THALIA These are my trainees

POLYKLEITOS What happened to your eyes?

HAEMON Nothing
They met some flying masonry
At high velocity
I was a student doctor
Now I'm this
Haemon

POLYKLEITOS Polykleitos
Forgive me if I ask what good will speaking do?

EUNOMIA Thalia's been taking testimony since the massacre

THALIA Before the war I was a social worker

EUNOMIA Now she's been elected Minister of Justice

THALIA I care about that word. I want to see it done

POLYKLEITOS Forgive me if I say I've heard it all before

HAEMON If this country is to heal, we have to start a dialogue between the victims of the violence and its perpetrators

THALIA We hear you've suffered loss

POLYKLEITOS Everyone has suffered loss

I've been working for the Athenians

As mechanic

Dismantling these weapons

It feels good.

Turn on your machine

HAEMON *starts recording.*

Before the war I had a garage

My son and me were hiding in the store.

In other countries, children are a precious thing.

In Thebes they have no value

I can't vomit up the words

THALIA Each child's death should bring this city to a halt

I lost my daughter in this war

POLYKLEITOS I spent my life in service to the gods

Not in service no, in contemplation of the mystery

I thought there was an order to the universe

When I looked up at the sky at night

I'd see a pattern mathematical in its complexity

Now I see random dots

There's nothing

But

An image like a bloodstain

Of the soldiers

Roaring through our streets.

Gunfire tore the air

The screams, the pleading

Opheltes my boy and me crouching down

The world held back with a flimsy door

I said we're safe in here

We're safe

A man broke down our door

His grin

HAEMON Do you remember when, which faction, which attack on Thebes?

POLYKLEITOS I know exactly who he was

That's why I'm speaking here.

He took my son and –

ELSEWHERE: **PRINCE TYDEUS** *enters.*

TYDEUS OK that's enough, don't look at them; you look at me. I'm more enlightening than anything that's going on there. That is sad old shit. Truth and reconciliation? That is sell your neighbour by a different name. That is make up lies about the people you don't like and get them tried for war crimes. I bet I'm being blamed for every murder here in Thebes and none of it is true, no, none of it. I am Prince Tydeus. Not a royal one; my mother brought me up to run her pig farm actually; it's just that Prince is quite a common name in Thebes – a lot of mothers like to have a little Prince. But I was never going to spend my life with swine. The gods had better plans for me. Now here are three true facts. One: I am a first class athlete. I have wiped the floor with all the best of Athens and with Sparta. I have won first prize at the Nemean Games. You can see my winning javelin throw on my own website – one of the first in Thebes – designed by the woman I adore, who understands domains

SENATOR PARGEIA *enters.*

Kids have posters of me on their walls draped in the flag of Thebes; Prince Tydeus; gold. Two: I have had communication with the gods

PARGEIA That's true

The Prince first saw Dionysus when he was just a little boy

TYDEUS I didn't see

It's more like I became

PARGEIA You hear that?

He becomes

Like in that movie where the man puts on the mask

TYDEUS Not quite like that

I felt him in me when I won that gold;

Felt him moving in me

When I led my men through Thebes.

I feel his light within my heart, my brain

I hear his holy laugh come out my mouth

I'll tell you this

Dionysus is a very complex god.

He doesn't choose just anyone

Three: I fought for justice and for peace

PARGEIA That's right. He fought for Polynices

TYDEUS He was rightful heir in Thebes and he should be running it right now. Polynices taught me everything I know. He was more like a brother than a friend. This is his wife, Pargeia

PARGEIA Hi

TYDEUS I was just telling them about your skill with websites and domains

PARGEIA That's nice

TYDEUS This woman is a true life heroine. Not only is she beautiful

PARGEIA Now now

TYDEUS But she is clever and she's full of heart

PARGEIA During the war years, while I worked as loan advisor at the bank of Thebes I used my post to raise funds for the orphans

TYDEUS Any other information you might hear about her finances is quite unfuckingtrue

PARGEIA My husband, Polynices should be ruling Thebes. But he
I'm sorry

TYDEUS He's among the disappeared

PARGEIA No he is not "among". He is unique. He has uniquely
gone. He led his men into the whirlwind of the fight and then

TYDEUS He has not been seen

PARGEIA Tydeus is my best support

My truest Prince

He has sat with me through my hours of grief

The torment of not knowing

TYDEUS We stood for Polynices in this election

PARGEIA Our policies were strong

Firm leadership

Security for all those on our side

TYDEUS But then we lost

It's inconfuckingceivable

We're merely senators

PARGEIA Which only goes to show how ludicrous elections are

THALIA approaches.

THALIA Senator Tydeus

TYDEUS That is Prince to you

She hands him a document.

THALIA The Truth and Reconciliation Commission of Thebes
requests you to appear before it to address yourself to
allegations of war crimes and gross human rights violations
during the course of the Theban Civil war. Failure to attend
will result in compulsory subpoena and criminal prosecution.
(to **PARGEIA***)* Good morning to you, Senator Pargeia. I hear
they are investigating loan frauds at the bank of Thebes. Have
a lovely day

She exits.

PARGEIA Hold back

Resist the rage

TYDEUS Fuck democracy. I hate the whole idea of it

We've got enough arms left to take the compound

And the palace –

PARGEIA Do I need to say it twice? Hold back

Sweet Prince

Sometimes you are an innocent.

There are much better ways to fuck those bitches up

TYDEUS When I look at you

It's like I feel the god

Rising up in me

He tries to kiss her. **ANTIGONE** *enters.*

PARGEIA I want to

But I can't

Not while my husband Polynices lives

She sees **ANTIGONE**, *who is looking at her strangely.*

Sister

I don't like the way you look at me

Like I'm not good enough

To be your brother's wife

And I have proved my worth

On my feet and on my back

Please tell me what your problem is

ANTIGONE The dead see everything we do

PARGEIA *exits.*

TYDEUS Oedipus' daughters

There are two

The mad one and the cute one.

This one's mad

He exits. **ANTIGONE** *remains.* **ISMENE** *enters.*

ACT TWO

Scene One
Investing

ISMENE What are you doing? What's the matter?

ANTIGONE They found Polynices. Dead

ISMENE I know
Antigone

ANTIGONE I went to look at him.
His eyes were no longer eyes
Open right into the deep

ISMENE He's dead and gone
It's over

As they speak the stage is being prepared for the inauguration.

ANTIGONE I'm going to anoint the corpse with oil
Come with me

ISMENE But it's Eurydice's inauguration

ANTIGONE Why should I care for that?

ISMENE She wants us with her, by her side

The company are entering and taking up position.

ANTIGONE But he's our brother

ISMENE You never lived with him. I did
You were on the road with Oedipus for all those years
And you were spared

ANTIGONE Spared? Out there in the war zone with our dying father?

ISMENE Polynices was a cunning, red-eyed despot

And this palace was a prison under him.

He used to pick up women from the town

And bring them here to play with and to rape.

You ask Eurydice. She hated him –

ANTIGONE I don't care what he did

ISMENE He let his generals

High on heroin and gunpowder

He let dogs like Prince Tydeus

ANTIGONE I've heard the stories same as you

ISMENE Stories?

ANTIGONE I've seen his necklace made of fingers

ISMENE I hated him

ANTIGONE He is our blood

ISMENE I won't go back

The war is over

ANTIGONE Not until we've buried all the dead.

I've noticed in these days of peace, how soon you have concerned yourself with what to wear, with grooming, painting of your toes –

ISMENE We have survived

Survived our lives so far.

Why not start living them?

ANTIGONE *cracks into tears.*

ANTIGONE We have to bury him

ISMENE Why?

ANTIGONE He frightens me

ISMENE *embraces her.*

The company enters, **TYDEUS** *and* **PARGEIA** *making a flamboyant show.*

TYDEUS Senators, good morning

ERIS What are you doing here?

PARGEIA We are elected representatives of Thebes

TYDEUS We're here to offer hospitality to Theseus

HELIA There's something here that you don't understand

EUPHROSYNE Called politics

THALIA We won the votes

We are the government

You lost

You are the opposition

PARGEIA So?

EUNOMIA You're not invited

AGLAEA Senators, your place is over there

> **PARGEIA** *and* **TYDEUS** *retreat to their positions. A rousing national anthem. The Athenians join in, unsure of tune or words.* **EURYDICE** *and* **THESEUS** *enter.*

ANTHEM In the towns and our plain lands

In the heart of our Thebes

The road to peace and freedom

Is a path for us all

For we will build a new world

Our nation will be reborn

And feel the pride of our plain lands

In the heart of our Thebes

> **EURYDICE** *stands at a podium,* **THESEUS** *at her side.*

> **ANTIGONE** *tries to leave.* **ISMENE** *holds her back. At last* **ANTIGONE** *acquiesces.*

The **ANTHEM** *ends.* **ANTIGONE,** *an oddity among the dignitaries, keeps her head bowed.*

EURYDICE Thebans, war is over. We are free.

How happy it makes me to say that.

Let me say it again loud and clear

People of Thebes, we are free.

This is truly a wonderful day.

I stand before you, leader of our new democracy.

My first task is to thank you

Thank you for believing Thebes can rise again

And thank you for believing in

This Theban woman. She believes in you.

I want to talk to the women here

The women in this city turned the tide for peace,

Women put themselves in danger

Walked wearing white in front of guns,

Nagged and pleaded, begged and laboured

Advocated tirelessly, withheld sexual favours

And never gave up. Women gave us peace.

This new administration will reflect their courage.

Women will be given prominence at every level.

Euphrosyne, Minister of Finance

Thalia, Minister of Justice

Aglaea, Foreign Secretary

Bia, Trade and Industry

Helia, Agriculture

Eris, Chief of Police

And men, we love you too:

Xenophanes, Education

We have senators reflecting all opinions here

Some radically different from my own.

We'll learn to listen, compromise and bend

We'll learn the skills of peace
Here, to share our celebration
Theseus, First Citizen of Athens.

THESEUS There is excitement in the air.

I can hear it, Thebans, feel it.
Like the rhythm of your famous music,
I find it irresistible. As I look down
Upon your city streets and out across
Your towns and fertile plains
I see you all rebuilding homes
Mending roads, reconstructing life.

I'm honoured to be witness at the birth of this democracy. When I return next time, I hope to see an open governmental infrastructure, functioning without corruption. I hope to see the rule of law. I hope to see a land where business thrives, endeavour is rewarded, and stability achieved. If peace is maintained, Athens and her partners could do business here. Imagine this: a vast economic development zone, bringing investment and employment; industry that would transform your land. The quality is there, the opportunity, the will. Your war is over. Now improve yourselves. Thank you

EURYDICE In our hope for the peace, let us not forget the war.

Thebes has been witness to atrocities
That I can hardly heave into my mouth
We have seen butchery and slaughter
Our girls raped, boys brutalised with guns.
What meaning can we find in that?
The only meaning is to make a lasting peace.
We have lost children, parents, brothers, sisters
I lost my husband Creon, Menoceus my youngest son,
My eldest, Haemon, blinded here

HAEMON Not blind

EURYDICE I fought with grief through the long night
And in your faces I can see its shadow.

I want to remember those we have lost.

Please join me in two minutes silence.

TIRESIAS *marks the beginning of the silence.*

All bow their heads. For the first time, ANTIGONE *raises hers. About thirty seconds pass.* TYDEUS *falls to his knees. He speaks in a high voice.*

TYDEUS People – For you I died

A long time I lay in darkness

Then the plates of my skull came apart

PARGEIA The dead speak

TYDEUS My spirit breathed

Began to rise

It ploughed the night sky

Searching for the hidden side

That keeps Elysium from human eyes

PARGEIA But far below where lies the plain of Thebes

There came a roar of souls

Thebes

We mourn for you

The dead are grieving

You have been robbed of strength

Your power is lost in woman's hands

Look to the p –

To the p

Look to the prince

TYDEUS *feigns collapse.*

TIRESIAS The dead are all around

You make a mockery of them

You deafen them

TIRESIAS *marks the end of the silence.*

THALIA / You have insulted the dead

EUPHROSYNE / You shameless fake

EURYDICE I know that violent men still lurk

Trying to spin their dark ideas aflame.

But while we breathe we will resist them

/ And we will not let you down

PARGEIA Thebes, her promises are hollow

/Eurydice can't keep control

EURYDICE I will not let you oppress and silence me

PARGEIA We need a powerful leader

You are standing in our place

EURYDICE Your president, people of Thebes

Will not be bullied or harassed

THESEUS Listen now

This is a democracy

And everybody gets a chance to speak.

That is what you have a senate for

PARGEIA Beloved Theseus, the dead have spoken here

TYDEUS Who did they die for?

Not Eurydice, not this

PARGEIA They died for Thebes

TYDEUS / Don't betray the Theban dead

Revolt against this government of women

EURYDICE I did not march into the guns of violent men

To then be cowed by them.

I will speak. I will speak. I will speak.

To reconcile does not mean to forget.

We must never forget,

Lest we make the same mistakes again.

Polynices' body has been found.

It will not be given burial

ANTIGONE *steps forward.* **PARGEIA** *almost collapses.*

This warlord's corpse shall be our monument

To all the horrors we have witnessed / and survived

PARGEIA If you don't bury him his soul will walk / the earth

EURYDICE His violent ideology will decompose –

As peace grows up and / overwhelms it

PARGEIA Polynices

EURYDICE The ground where he lies

It will be a garden of / reflection

Where we can meditate upon the cost of war

TYDEUS People, to the square, come now

Come in your multitudes

If you have human feeling then oppose this wrong

PARGEIA Polynices

PARGEIA's *distress is epic.* **TYDEUS** *escorts her out.*

EURYDICE I love Thebes.

I see light. I see water

I see the terror melting like ice

Let us turn away from shadows.

If you oppose me, tell me democratically.

Work hard for peace

Be part of this great effort.

Join hands, be free

THESEUS May I?

EURYDICE Thank you

THESEUS *leads* **EURYDICE** *down from the podium.*

ANTIGONE Her first act as all-powerful ruler is to let our brother
rot

ISMENE Antigone

THESEUS An interesting speech, ma'am

ISMENE She is not the monster

EURYDICE Thank you

ISMENE Don't go

THESEUS I should offer you the service of my writing team. They're very good at rousing with the facts

EURYDICE That's very kind

THESEUS You know, an expert on language and the human brain said that women find rhetoric more difficult

EURYDICE Thank you very much for telling me

THESEUS I mean next time, before you go up there, you could run your stuff by my professionals to see if there's improvements to be made / because

EURYDICE I write my own words, thank you. My late husband Creon said it was statesmanship

THESEUS Statesmanship, that's nice. That decomposing corpse

EURYDICE Polynices

THESEUS You should have run that by me

EURYDICE I didn't know the dead were an Athenian concern.
Forgive my inexperience

THESEUS *(to PHAEAX)* The possessed guy

PHAEAX That was Prince Tydeus; electoral opponent

THESEUS And she?

PHAEAX Senator Pargeia. She's the corpse's wife

TALTHYBIA You'll find detailed profiles of them in my briefing, sir

PHAEAX She used to be a dancer

THESEUS Fascinating

PHAEAX He's the guy who won at the Nemean games

THESEUS Impassioned, isn't he?

PHAEAX His record for the javelin still stands

THESEUS OK. His name again

PHAEAX Tydeus

THESEUS The prince. *(to* **EURYDICE***)* He is a tough adversary

EURYDICE Yes, and so am I.

This is my son, Haemon

THESEUS How do you do?

HAEMON I started my medical training in Athens; beautiful city

THESEUS Certainly is

HAEMON I mean what are your plans

Sorry to jump on you like this but

Healthcare provision

We need drugs, buildings, trained staff

/ It's critical that –

PHAEAX The provision of medical aid is a topic for discussion tomorrow. It will receive our full attention then

THESEUS What happened to your eyes?

HAEMON Nothing

EURYDICE He was / injured

HAEMON I've suffered certain functional changes but

EURYDICE He's blind

HAEMON Why do you keep –

I'm not blind.

I can see your dress

That thing you're wearing on your head

I can see Antigone

He is pointing at **ISMENE***.*

My sight is just impaired

THESEUS That happen in the war?

HAEMON In the peace

Clearing rubble from our disused university

One of the factions had it booby trapped with mines

THESEUS I'm very sorry

HAEMON Yes. They were Athenian-made

EURYDICE Haemon

HAEMON That's the irony you see. Thebes is not a weapons-manufacturing state. Most of the arms in our conflict were / Athenian

EURYDICE My nieces; Ismene, Antigone

THESEUS Your father was Oedipus, right

ISMENE That's right

ANTIGONE Our father and our brother

He shakes **ISMENE**'s *hand.*

THESEUS Yes. I feel I'm shaking hands with someone destiny has touched. You're Antigone?

ISMENE Ismene

THESEUS There are some families like that

Families who get touched by destiny

Chosen in some way –

Don't you think so?

ANTIGONE / Yes

ISMENE No, I don't

EURYDICE My cabinet in waiting; Euphrosyne, Minister of Finance

PHAEAX The teacher

EUPHROSYNE How do you do?

THESEUS My pleasure

EUPHROSYNE I have the honour of holding the purse strings of a bankrupt state. I've explored the lining of this purse in case a coin or two is hiding there but all I've found is fluff and old receipts

THESEUS That's too bad

EUPHROSYNE I also have a cheque for you; the latest instalment of interest on the overwhelming debts we have inherited. Would you like it?

PHAEAX Debt relief is down on the conference agenda but there are various criteria you must fulfil and now is not the time to list them

PHAEAX *doesn't take the cheque.*

EURYDICE Eris, Chief of Police

THESEUS How do you –

ERIS We're going to have the rule of law here

But we need to retrain, reorganise

We can make Thebes safe

But we need your cash

EURYDICE Xenophanes, education

THESEUS Very nice to –

XENOPHANES We have to re-educate our men

A generation now thinks rape and looting is their right.

Education is the road to change

But it's expensive –

EURYDICE Thalia, Minister of Justice

THALIA We have so much to talk about. A just society – how is that achievable?

THESEUS Well

THALIA I hope that Thebes can learn from your mistakes

EUPHROSYNE He looks like a movie star doesn't he?

THALIA You have the figure and the bearing of a very gifted actor

EURYDICE Aglaea, Foreign Minister

THESEUS How do you do?

AGLAEA We met before. I came to Athens just before the massacre to plead for intervention

THESEUS That's right

AGLAEA Sadly it was not forthcoming

EURYDICE We've arranged a Theban feast. We hope you'll join us

PHAEAX Sir, our caterers have worked alongside theirs to ensure health and hygiene

THESEUS Thank you, Madam President

> **EURYDICE** *and* **THESEUS** *exit with* **PHAEAX** *and the senators.*

TALTHYBIA *(to* **AGLAEA***)* I have to say it isn't wise. Please tell your people. Don't make Theseus feel that he's at fault. He didn't make this war

> *They exit.* **ISMENE** *and* **ANTIGONE** *alone.*

ANTIGONE I'm going to bury him, Ismene

ISMENE Can't you see there's something more important going on?

ANTIGONE His soul can't rest

ISMENE If you bury him now you'll be siding with Tydeus and the widow

ANTIGONE / No I won't

ISMENE They'll leap on you like a trophy. / They'll use you, Antigone

ANTIGONE This has got nothing to do with Prince Tydeus or anyone else

ISMENE It has to do with all of Thebes. We have to be so careful

ANTIGONE Why?

ISMENE Because of who we are

ANTIGONE Last remnants of a cursed house

ISMENE I want to represent the future not the past. We must embrace this peace

ANTIGONE Eurydice isn't peace

She's power

Power is never peace

It is barbarity.

Come with me

ISMENE Why don't we talk to her?

She's not / unreasonable

ANTIGONE What good did talking ever do?

The only thing to do is act – and you

Have never done

Anything

HAEMON enters. They both look at him; **ISMENE** *with a certain amount of hope.*

HAEMON Antigone?

ISMENE immediately leaves.

Where are you going? Don't go

ANTIGONE I'm here

HAEMON My mother asks if you'll come in and join the feast

ANTIGONE I'm not hungry

HAEMON Antigone

ANTIGONE Don't come too near

HAEMON Why not?

ANTIGONE I'm ill

HAEMON What with?

ANTIGONE Don't know

HAEMON I know what I must seem; how especially

Disgusting my fading sight must seem

ANTIGONE To me?

HAEMON I wish it was an arm or leg

But it's my eyes. My images of you

Are stuck now in the past. I doubt I'll see

Your face again though I imagine it.

Are you still there?

ANTIGONE Yes

HAEMON It's common to feel

Paranoid like that, they say.

I think that I see people creep away.

They've warned me of hallucinations too.

I might see any nonsense, any lie

And take it for what's real. Don't go

ANTIGONE I'm not

HAEMON This is a minor injury in Theban terms –

ANTIGONE You're not especially disgusting

Why did you say that?

HAEMON Before I went to Athens I remember you

Leading your blind father

Seeing for him, so small

You were like a bird

Taking him where you found interest

Even if he didn't want to go.

I loved to watch.

You were a proper child

You had a playful spirit

Your smile could penetrate his blindness

Wrap itself around his grief

You were his light, Antigone.

I've always felt it when I looked at you

Some kind of light

Don't know why

You're scrawny, awkward

Not like Ismene she is radiant I'd say but you

You're like a flare burning through the night.

Since I've been like this it's you I've seen

Your face, your eyes, those eyes.

He reaches out for her.

Are you still here?

ANTIGONE I thought it was Ismene that you loved

HAEMON It's you

They touch.

ANTIGONE I'm dangerous to touch

HAEMON Like fire

ANTIGONE I'm ill

HAEMON What with?

ANTIGONE Don't know

HAEMON Do you feel anything for me?

ANTIGONE No

Suddenly she is in his arms.

HAEMON I knew

I knew you did

ANTIGONE Help me

HAEMON Antigone

Late at night. **MILETUS, SCUD** *and* **MEGAERA** *are guarding the body of Polynices.* **HARMONIA** *is quietly singing.*

MEGAERA More dishonest work for warriors to do

MILETUS If we're told to sit here with a stiff, we sit with it. That way
   we get fed

SCUD This kid that I was with

   Don't know his name but he was small

   A green militia came with faces painted white

   We found him lying there

   After the bullets and the fight

   His life had gone – but there was not a scratch on him

MEGAERA Another dead kid story from the Junior Lieutenant

SCUD He died of fear the big men said

   And they pissed on him.

   I didn't know that it was possible

   To die from fear

   He followed us for some time after that

   And he was grey

   Once he touched me on the back

MEGAERA That's nice of him. That's friendly isn't it – shut up

   EURYDICE *and* **THESEUS** *lead the company out from dinner.*
   HARMONIA *begs.*

EURYDICE When Cadmus founded Thebes

   He laid Harmonia, his beloved, in their bed

   And drew the seven gates around her

   Taking his inspiration from the seven heavens.

   Thebes is laid out like a celestial map

45

THESEUS That's poetic. Athens is a grid

EURYDICE Our districts have the names of constellations

That's Lyra Town down there

And over here on the hill is the spring where Cadmus killed the giant serpent

THESEUS Wow

EURYDICE He threw its teeth on the ground and warriors sprang up

They helped him build the city

EURYDICE and **THESEUS** *move away, followed by* **PHAEAX**, *aides and bodyguards and senators.* **THALIA, EUPHROSYNE** *and* **BIA** *remain.*

THALIA She's doing very well

BIA That charm of hers. She makes it look so easy

THALIA Perhaps it is to her

EUPHROSYNE These Athenians. We speak the same language; we have the same gods but they're so hard to talk to. I felt like an anthropologist in there

HELIA They've got no sense of humour

EUPHROSYNE I was with that aide

HELIA Oh he's a nightmare

EUPHROSYNE I couldn't think of anything to say

I found myself describing the destruction of my village

His eyes glazed over straight away, the food stayed on his plate

Then I remembered sport –

Thank the gods he talked for half an hour

THALIA That girl with the unusual hair –

BIA Talthybia

HELIA She knocked her drink into her lap

THALIA Poor thing

She asked so many questions

I was actually impressed

I think she's a bit in love with Theseus

BIA So am I

EUPHROSYNE Well I'm sorry to inform you that he has a wife

BIA No match for me

AGLAEA *enters.*

EUPHROSYNE A beautiful young wife; Phaedra. Their wedding was all over the celebrity sites on the internet. Of course I never look at them. But her dress; so many little precious stones sewn into the organza. You could open several schools for what it cost

AGLAEA Can't we rise above the gossip?

EUPHROSYNE This isn't gossip, this is economics

AGLAEA Listen

That's Pargeia and the prince down in the square

I've told Eris to stand by with her police

What if there's trouble and they can't contain it?

THALIA We have the peacekeepers

It's what they're here for

BIA We'll go and talk to their security

BIA *and* **HELIA** *exit.*

EUPHROSYNE I don't think Tydeus will attempt a coup while Theseus is here

AGLAEA Tydeus wants to show him we're unstable and incapable

He wants to show we're overwhelmed / by the task

EUPHROSYNE Overwhelmed but undaunted. We're planting seeds here ladies; tiny seeds that will grow and change the land

THALIA The Athenians are pulling out in ten days time. We have to have assurances of aid and debt relief. Eurydice has got to sell us hard

AGLAEA How I hate the fact that we need Theseus.

That speech of his

It made me livid

Telling us we could improve ourselves

As if we're children learning how to spell

And offering the carrot of his economic zone

EUPHROSYNE He's got to feed the great Athenian god; the god of profit

AGLAEA And Eurydice – I'm sorry but I'm furious.

What was she thinking of – to leave that corpse exposed without discussion and without advice?

EUPHROSYNE Your voice is very loud

AGLAEA That rabble in the square; she's given them the gift of self-righteous indignation. What an error – and she made it like an autocrat

THALIA You see the thing is, I appreciate her gesture. I lost my daughter in this war

AGLAEA I know, I know –

THALIA And that unburied monster –

I know it wasn't him that raped and killed her

But the fact that there's just one,

Just one of those ferocious men

Whose soul will never rest

AGLAEA You're Minister of Justice

THALIA Yes I think that it is just.

His corpse is made to pay

The dead make reparation

While the living start to heal

EUPHROSYNE We have to show her loyalty

AGLAEA What of her loyalty to us?

We senators must act as a control on her great power

EUPHROSYNE We need her to have power.

What good is honest, competent committee
In the face of Prince Tydeus?
He genuinely thinks that he's a god.
And he is charismatic, handsome, plausible
Especially with that glossy thief upon his arm.
We're dull, we're ageing, we wear comfy footwear
None of us is sexy any more
We don't throw parties, we like gardening

AGLAEA Tydeus and Pargeia have the crowd
We have to hope that when the food and beer runs out
Their cult of character will sour

THALIA We must have Theseus

EUPHROSYNE And to get him we need her, Eurydice
Her confidence, her charm, her gravitas
Her sense of her own right –

AGLAEA Her pride

EUPHROSYNE Your pride

THALIA We have to be united. Please stand firm
Or the approaching rush
Will overwhelm us all

EUPHROSYNE The greatest threat to Thebes
Is Thebes itself

PHAEAX *and* **ENYALIUS** *enter with the senators.*

PHAEAX Excuse me, what is going on down there?

AGLAEA Keep calm

PHAEAX I have concerns for Theseus

AGLAEA Keep calm
We should stand by
But not provoke
That way this little fire will burn itself right out

Exit aides and senators.

ELSEWHERE: *the revellers enter, carrying* **TYDEUS** *on their shoulders.* **POLYKLEITOS** *watches from the shadows.*

TYDEUS Breathe frenzy

PARGEIA Prince Tydeus

A chant starts up: 'Breathe frenzy, **PRINCE TYDEUS.** '

POLYKLEITOS *raises a gun; aims it at* **TYDEUS.**

TYDEUS Breathe frenzy

POLYKLEITOS *cannot pull the trigger. He lowers the gun. The revellers exit.*

ELSEWHERE: **TALTHYBIA** *is with* **ISMENE.**

TALTHYBIA I've drunk too much

ISMENE Me too

TALTHYBIA What is that stuff, that wine?

ISMENE Not really wine. It's made out of fermented bread

TALTHYBIA Oh, fermented

THESEUS *enters. He is on his mobile phone.*

THESEUS Can you do something for me please?
Call in on your mother? Yes I know she is;
I mean on Phaedra she's your mother now

TALTHYBIA Great sky

ISMENE You have the same sky over Athens

THESEUS / I'm only asking you to see if she's OK
She hasn't been returning calls
I don't know what she's doing there

TALTHYBIA Our sky's polluted with a smog of light
/But that is just spectacular. That path

THESEUS I'm worried that –

Just go

Find out why she's there. And privately –

ISMENE Oh yes, the path of stars

THESEUS You keep it in the family. Thanks.

TALTHYBIA At first I thought it was a kind of high cloud cover but this Theban guy I met who dismantles guns and weapons said it's actually

POLYKLEITOS *(elsewhere)* / The Milky Way

TALTHYBIA The Milky Way

ISMENE That's right

TALTHYBIA I didn't know. He said our star, the sun

POLYKLEITOS Is on an outer spur of a great spiral of the galaxy

TALTHYBIA And the Milky Way

POLYKLEITOS Or silver river, is our view of the

Galactic plane going right into the crux

Full of dust from old, exploded stars

And ionising new ones – countless

Suns and moons and planets and it turns

Through space at an amazing speed, not just

A moon around an earth or earth round sun

But all of it; the galaxy spins round

TALTHYBIA And this mechanic guy said it's just one

POLYKLEITOS Of billions like it in the universe

TALTHYBIA And at the centre of it all, guess what

He was looking for?

ISMENE A supermassive black hole

TALTHYBIA No, not that. He said he wanted Heaven

ISMENE Very nice

POLYKLEITOS / Elysium

TALTHYBIA Elysium; that was the word he used.

He searches for Elysium

ISMENE The centre of the galaxy is actually dark matter

TALTHYBIA Oh. OK

ISMENE It's going to eat us up

THESEUS She's right. One day you'd better hope

You're on a space ship out of here

He laughs. No one else finds it funny. **EURYDICE** *enters;* **AGLAEA**
and **ERIS** *are briefing her.*

I used to do a lot of sailing;

Love the night sky

And I'm appreciating what you said about dark matter

I've read a lot about black holes and stuff, Antigone.

Dark matter means we've got to make the most of what's
around

AGLAEA *and* **ERIS** *exit.* **EURYDICE** *approaches.*

EURYDICE We've had a small disturbance in the central square

It's calming down

THESEUS Your opposition, right?

EURYDICE Just drunken revellers

Celebrating our democracy

THESEUS Making their feelings known about the dead guy

EURYDICE That is their democratic right

THESEUS *(to* **TALTHYBIA***)* Could we get some music here?

I hate an evening without music

ISMENE In Thebes we always make our own

She exits, with **TALTHYBIA**.

EURYDICE You don't like silence, Theseus?

THESEUS You don't like music?

EURYDICE Did you make your call?

THESEUS Yes thank you. My wife has left our place in Athens and she's heading for the coast. Why would she do that?

EURYDICE I don't know

THESEUS Hippolytus my son is stationed there with his battalion. I've asked him to go out and check on her

EURYDICE That's very good of him

THESEUS He doesn't like her. Not one bit.

I'm not entirely sure that he likes me

EURYDICE Families can be very difficult

THESEUS You lost a son, is that right?

EURYDICE He

Down by the walls

Menoceus, my youngest.

In an ambush

He was

Pause.

THESEUS How did you lose your husband?

EURYDICE On his way to Delphi at one of our outlying villages, his convoy was stopped at a roadblock. It was made of human intestines

THESEUS No way

EURYDICE They were massacred

THESEUS By this Polynices?

EURYDICE By his men. I don't think they knew who Creon was. They were just massacring everyone that day. But when they realised who they'd killed they – let's say they made full use of his remains

THESEUS What happens when a whole state

When a place descends into – Fuck

It's like you bred some different kind of war out here

EURYDICE All war is savage Theseus, whether it's fought close
quarters with machetes or from afar with missiles and computer
guided bombs. Are you more civilized because you can't hear
people scream?

THESEUS Your war was bestial

EURYDICE Our war was very human

THESEUS Then I fear a new breed of mankind. Men with no
feeling, no idea of order or regard for any tie, men whose only
motivation is the basest lust for power

EURYDICE That's new?

THESEUS The path we've been on for the last millennium or so,
the glory of the city state, philosophy and science, freedom,
art, enlightenment; the things that Athens stands for. I believe
in them and I had thought our progress irreversible. I thought
we would continue to evolve towards the gods

EURYDICE We're not evolving backwards here

THESEUS What happened? How did this exterminating butchery
take hold?

EURYDICE It could happen anywhere

THESEUS You cannot say that

EURYDICE Does it frighten you?

Do you think we brought it on ourselves?

It could happen anywhere where there is tyranny.

You should go out and talk to people, talk

As I have done to those who have endured.

I'd say they were the finest human beings you could meet.

What's happened here is in the past.

Perhaps you are afraid of us

Because the chaos here, the great descent

Just might be in your future

THESEUS What the hell makes you say that?

EURYDICE An observation, merely

ISMENE *and* **TALTHYBIA** *enter with a clockwork radio. Music.*

TALTHYBIA Some music, sir

EURYDICE Thank you, Talthybia. Good night

TALTHYBIA *and* **ISMENE** *exit.*

THESEUS I've made an observation too. You have a way with people that I envy; got them wrapped around your finger

EURYDICE Have I?

THESEUS You appear strong

EURYDICE I'm motivated by necessity

THESEUS You appear humane, intelligent, compassionate and wise. But I'm not sure if you are

EURYDICE Thebes knows what I stand for and the people trust me to bring change. It's what I must do – or die trying

THESEUS That's so Theban, bringing death into every sentence

EURYDICE Death is everywhere in Thebes

THESEUS Like your address; way too dramatic. Some of the things you said

EURYDICE I said we must reconcile

THESEUS No, you said light and water and men lurking in the dark spinning fire

EURYDICE All the most important things were said

THESEUS This dead boy that you refuse to bury

EURYDICE The warlord who murdered my son

THESEUS Where does he fit in to your reconciliation?

EURYDICE I explained that in my speech

THESEUS His corpse will be a theme park?

EURYDICE Don't misinterpret me. It's vital to the healing of our wounds that he makes reparation. I've no desire to clash with you

THESEUS Quite right

EURYDICE But this is Theban business. You've no right to interfere

THESEUS May I just say how well you argue and defend yourself.
For someone new to government, you're good

EURYDICE Thank you

THESEUS You're also beautiful

EURYDICE I – what?

THESEUS That is so unusual in politics
Not coming on to you; just stating a bare fact.
Beauty is a very powerful thing.
My wife is beautiful
Phaedra; gets mistaken for my daughter.
Don't know why I'm saying this
Relief perhaps
Of being with a woman my own age
A clever, charming, deeply foreign woman
Pause.

EURYDICE Thank you but we have no electricity
No schools, no medicine, no roads
No jobs, no drinking water
Children dying in their droves
Our life expectancy is thirty eight.
I'm old beyond my years

THESEUS You don't look old.
I envy you, you know
Envy the adventure, the extremity
Our lives in Athens seem mundane
We have no tragedy. And tragedy
Reminds us how to live

EURYDICE I'm glad it serves some purpose

THESEUS Eurydice. You'll learn how rare it is to meet an equal

EURYDICE Theseus, my hands are tied with monstrous poverty.

For Thebes to thrive where chaos gaped and roared

You can perform that miracle –

THESEUS You see this is what I'm saying; metaphors and monsters.
Gaped and roared; that's just verbose. It's / not effective

EURYDICE What I have said is very clear. We need a future. You can
/ help us

THESEUS You've just been elected.

I can see you're very keen.

But this is stuff for conference tomorrow

EURYDICE Our time together is so brief

/ Forgive me if

THESEUS You are a natural and I'm most impressed.

But sometimes late at night

When everything official has been said

We leaders of the world like to

Take off the mask

We've done the altruism and diplomacy.

Now let's do something else

EURYDICE What would amuse you, Theseus?

THESEUS Like look up at the stars

And see what destiny might hold

EURYDICE It's worrying that you don't listen. Is it something that
the male brain has inadequate equipment for?

THESEUS I do listen and I think you're so naive. There is a lot that
I could do for Thebes

EURYDICE Naive?

THESEUS But let's remember that essentially you're begging here,
you're on your knees

EURYDICE That's what I've said. Thebes is / imprisoned by

THESEUS Not Thebes; you. Every thousand that I pledge keeps you
in power. I just offered you equality

EURYDICE Did you?

THESEUS I had a glimpse of something just back then

Some sort of –

Obviously not destiny but say

A door swinging open unexpectedly.

This relationship with Thebes

Could be a pleasure not a chore

EURYDICE Are you

Are you suggesting

That we presidents

THESEUS I'm not a president; I'm just First Citizen

EURYDICE That's right, the common man

THESEUS Dionysus; he was born here, wasn't he, the God of wine?
Don't you women have a dance for him, some sort of rite?

EURYDICE Which guide book have you read?

THESEUS I'd like to see it.

Would you dance for me?

Pause.

What's up? I'm asking you to dance with me

EURYDICE You said for, dance for you

THESEUS I said to dance

EURYDICE I'm sorry but that isn't / what I heard

THESEUS Don't apologise

EURYDICE I'm not

THESEUS No seriously don't apologise

In politics, you can't admit mistakes

EURYDICE I haven't made one

THESEUS You cannot be wrong

EURYDICE I know that

THESEUS So then. What are you afraid of? Dance

Neither moves.

First light. **MILETUS** *and* **MEGAERA** *sleep.* **ANTIGONE** *is performing burial rites. She picks up a handful of dust. She lets it fall through her fingers over the corpse. She repeats the gesture.* **JUNIOR LIEUTENANT SCUD** *is watching her, curiously.* **MEGAERA** *wakes.*

ANTIGONE I lead the blind

I bury the dead

I follow the path

I am Antigone

MEGAERA *raises her gun. She aims it at* **ANTIGONE**.

MEGAERA Woosh

ACT THREE

SCENE ONE
Terrorising

TIRESIAS *enters with* HARMONIA. ISMENE *is making coffee – a ceremony over charcoal.*

TIRESIAS The ghosts

Their parched tongues are flickering

Like unseen negatives upon the day.

They form another city all round us

ISMENE I'm not afraid of you Tiresias.

You're like an old pet snake

Kept more out of pity than from fear

HARMONIA *holds out her hand.* ISMENE *gives her a coin.*

This girl you've stolen from her mother

Any day now she'll be going to school.

You're irrelevant in our new Thebes

TIRESIAS The dead are not irrelevant. They're here

THESEUS *enters, with* PHAEAX *and* TALTHYBIA. EURYDICE *enters with her ministers.*

EURYDICE Good morning

THESEUS Madam President

EURYDICE You must try our Theban coffee

THESEUS I did

EURYDICE Shall we begin our conference?

THESEUS There are people here who eat each other's brains, people who believe that snakes can change your gender. There are people who make roadblocks out of human innards, people who leave corpses right outside their gates. Are you ready for a place at the table?

EURYDICE How's your wife this morning, have you managed to get hold of her?

THESEUS My wife is not up for discussion here

He exits into the palace with **PHAEAX, TALTHYBIA** *and retinue.*

EUPHROSYNE What happened to him?

EURYDICE We'll start proceedings with your presentations

XENOPHANES I don't think that's Theseus' plan

HELIA Look at this agenda they've just given us

They've not scheduled any time for presentations

BIA In five years we could be standing on our feet

If he will only listen

EURYDICE We'll start as we intended

ERIS His men are armed you know

EURYDICE They're bodyguards not warlords

ERIS There should be no weapons

XENOPHANES No more discussion

Let's take the floor

They exit. **EURYDICE** *holds back* **THALIA, EUPHROSYNE** *and* **AGLAEA. EUNOMIA** *also remains.*

EURYDICE I have offended him

THALIA How?

EUPHROSYNE Child, whatever did you say?

EURYDICE It isn't what I said

It isn't anything I did

AGLAEA He made a pass at you

EUNOMIA I don't believe it

EURYDICE He said that he was offering equality

AGLAEA The hound

EURYDICE He said he envied me

He asked me what I was afraid of

EUPHROSYNE Oh gods you turned him down

THALIA You have insulted him

EURYDICE Maybe he was trying to make a link

To get beneath the mask

Perhaps I misinterpreted –

He didn't mean it as an insult –

Offered me an intimacy

AGLAEA He just can't keep it zipped up in his suit

THALIA Don't be flippant

AGLAEA This isn't flippancy

THALIA She has insulted the first citizen of / Athens

EUPHROSYNE Gods

What can we do?

We must have his / goodwill

THALIA You can't pretend you didn't see it coming

You were flirting with him

All that stuff about the / seven heavens

AGLAEA She had assumed equality, respect.

She didn't realise these were gifts to be bestowed by him

EURYDICE He'll mow me down in there

He'll dance all over me

The fate of Thebes hangs in the balance

AGLAEA Thebes the beggar, yes;

Not Thebes the whore.

Well done

You'll make a leader yet

THALIA Sister

Words said in haste

EURYDICE *reaches for the senators.*

EURYDICE I think

Under all the swagger

He's incredibly alone

And he can't communicate

AGLAEA Are you seriously pitying him?

EUPHROSYNE If it was me

I must confess

I'd have that suit off in a minute

AGLAEA You get in there

Exploit his weaknesses as he would exploit yours

Now take a big deep breath

EURYDICE *and* **AGLAEA** *exit into the palace.*

Let's have some coffee in there, child

THALIA Our work is cut out now

TYDEUS *enters with* **PARGEIA.**

EUNOMIA What do you want here?

PARGEIA We're coming to the conference

So make way

THALIA Let me explain one more time

You are the opposition

TYDEUS So?

EUNOMIA Go away

They exit.

TYDEUS Opposition, yes

Let's muster it

The men want action

PARGEIA Will you hold back?

If we start an insurrection

The Athenians will crush it.

We need them on our side

We have to get to Theseus

ISMENE *has finished the coffee. She prepares to take it in.*

TYDEUS Look at this, Pargeia

It's a real princess

PARGEIA Forget that stuck-up little virgin

TYDEUS That's no virgin

It's an inbred royal

ISMENE You're an embarrassment to Thebes

PARGEIA Your own brother

My dead husband lies unburied.

This is the embarrassment to Thebes

And you, his sister, you do / nothing

ISMENE Nothing, I do nothing, no

PARGEIA *(to* **TYDEUS***)* Come here

We are getting in this conference

Now

PARGEIA *exits.*

TYDEUS I like the way you keep our special secret.

I hear rape's a designated war crime now

And so I guess if you'd felt raped

You would have told.

Pleases me you treasure it.

You drew my blood

Kicking up against me in the dust.

Your teeth tore through my hand

You see that little scar?

My royal souvenir

ISMENE Get back

TYDEUS Bet there's no other man

Who makes your heartbeat race like that

TYDEUS tries to touch her. ISMENE pours the coffee on him.

Bitch

You're lucky all is peaceful now

You're lucky I'm so full of love

PARGEIA *(re-enters)* Have I been talking to myself? I said get in

TYDEUS Look at my fucking suit

PARGEIA What did you do to him, you clumsy little slut? You keep away

PARGEIA pushes ISMENE. HAEMON enters.

You and your sister and your motherfucking dad

She spits. Then exits with TYDEUS.

ISMENE tries to compose herself.

HAEMON Antigone, where did you go?

Last night I woke and you were gone

ISMENE No

HAEMON Why did you run away?

ISMENE / It's not –

HAEMON Listen, let me say it, marry me

I love you more than anyone

You're passionate

And dazzling

And good and

All that grief

If it is loved

If you are loved

It won't hurt so unremittingly.

Please be my wife

ISMENE *exits.* **TIRESIAS** *is amused.*

Antigone, Antigone

TIRESIAS Welcome to the country of the blind

MEGAERA, MILETUS *and* **SCUD** *enter with* **ANTIGONE,** *bound.*

MILETUS *(to* **HAEMON***)* We need to see Eurydice

HAEMON Who are you?

MEGAERA Her men

MILETUS We have a prisoner for her

HAEMON Who?

MEGAERA You can see for yourself

HAEMON *exits, without seeing* **ANTIGONE.**

MILETUS They might reward us

SCUD Who?

MILETUS The ones who gave us all a vote

SCUD I didn't vote

MILETUS You're only old enough to kill, not vote

ANTIGONE It's coming

My destiny

Swooping through the air

Atoms heavy with intention

MEGAERA Shut your face

ANTIGONE The blow will hit me

Take me off my feet

SCUD What blow?

ANTIGONE I am ready

SCUD What are atoms?

MILETUS Don't be talking to her Junior Lieutenant; she is nuts

SCUD She's right. There's something here

MEGAERA No Scud

SCUD *(raising his gun)* I can feel it; something bad

MEGAERA What are you, a dog?
You think you sense things humans can't?
Resist the madness, friend

ANTIGONE You should have let me bury him

MEGAERA You shut your face

SCUD It's like when those trees bent over us
The day my sister's spine was shot

MILETUS Don't think of it, Lieutenant

SCUD The trees bent forward / whispering

MILETUS You were twisted up with drugs

SCUD It was the shadow ones

> **TALTHYBIA** *enters followed by* **ISMENE**.

ISMENE I had the coffee made but then –

> **ISMENE** *stops, seeing* **ANTIGONE**.

> **TALTHYBIA** *crosses behind* **SCUD** *dressed in grey. He spins round, sees her. He instantly has his gun trained on her.*

SCUD GHOST
GET DOWN
GHOST

TALTHYBIA *squirms on the floor.* **ISMENE** *exits back into the palace.*

ISMENE EURYDICE

MILETUS Don't shoot

/ Don't shoot

ISMENE / EURYDICE

SCUD DON'T MOVE

MEGAERA / That is not a shadow

The company enters from the palace.

TYDEUS What the fuck / is this?

MILETUS Scud, if you shoot her, we will be at war again

SCUD / We are at war

EUPHROSYNE What's happening here?

MILETUS At peace, Scud. / This is peace

ERIS Thebans, put down your guns

THALIA / Oh Gods

Oh Gods

EURYDICE *and* **THESEUS** *enter;* **PHAEAX** *behind them with* **ENYALIUS, PLAUTUS** *and* **ICHNAEA,** *armed.*

ENYALIUS Put down the gun or we will take you out

ERIS / That is not the way

MEGAERA You take him out and I will kill this bitch down dead

ENYALIUS Plautus – cover her

ERIS / No guns

No guns

PHAEAX / Put the gun down, move away

MEGAERA *has her gun pointed at* **ANTIGONE.**

PLAUTUS *(to* **MEGAERA***)* One inch and I will kill you

ISMENE Antigone

/ Antigone

MEGAERA I am fury

ANTIGONE NO

THESEUS What's happened here?

ENYALIUS Sir please step back into the building

MILETUS No one move

ENYALIUS Step back into the building , sir

ICHNAEA Talthybia you're fine

EURYDICE What's happened here?

THESEUS You need to get back in the building

MILETUS We caught her burying the dead

EURYDICE / Antigone

TALTHYBIA I haven't buried / anyone

SCUD Shut up

/ Shut up

THESEUS Her name – quick

ICHNAEA Talthybia

THESEUS It's OK, Talthybia

TALTHYBIA OK, OK

SCUD Shut up you stay there

ISMENE Antigone what have you done?

> **EURYDICE** *is approaching* **SCUD** *like a woman who has walked into gunfire before.*

EURYDICE No one here will harm you soldier

Please put down the gun

THESEUS Now listen –

> **MILETUS** *aims his gun at* **THESEUS.**

MILETUS Don't move

The Junior Lieutenant is my responsibility.

NO ONE MOVE

THESEUS *is frozen.*

Scud look at me

(to **SCUD***)* She's not a ghost

She is Athenian

Touch her

SCUD *touches* **TALTHYBIA**. **EURYDICE** *slowly sits on the ground in front of him.*

SCUD We came to speak to someone

EURYDICE I am someone. Speak to me

SCUD Somebody who matters

TALTHYBIA She is the

SCUD Shut your mouth you bitch or I will shoot

EURYDICE I am Eurydice, your President.

There is no need for violence here

Let's all put down the guns

SCUD *lowers his gun.* **THESEUS***' aides do not lower theirs – neither does* **MEGAERA***.*

MILETUS OK, I'm lowering my gun

The Junior Lieutenant was mistaken, simply.

He means no one any harm

THESEUS *starts to breathe again.*

THESEUS I thought this palace was secure

PHAEAX / These are palace guards, sir

They're supposed to be security

ERIS You brought guns into a conference of peace

THESEUS How close are we here to being terrorised and shot?

EURYDICE This is one random action

THESEUS So is the death of every president

ICHNAEA Talthybia stay down

TALTHYBIA I'm fine, I'm cool, I'm desperately OK

ICHNAEA *(to* **MILETUS***)* DON'T MOVE

MILETUS Scud, tell them what we came for

> **PLUTUS** *changes position.*

MEGAERA Don't move or I will kill her

SCUD We were guarding someone. They were dead

MILETUS Polynices

SCUD Half the sky was black
The other half was blue and clear

MILETUS You tell them why we're here

SCUD That girl was digging, giving him the rites

PARGEIA Antigone

SCUD The earth was ready for him. Deep
Below me I could feel it gaping wide

EURYDICE What is your name?

> *The* **JUNIOR LIEUTENANT** *tries to remember it.*

MILETUS We call him Junior Lieutenant Scud

EURYDICE We can choose the dark black sky
Or chase the coming blue
Another life awaits you, my young son.
I pray it starts today
May blessings be upon you

> **MEGAERA** *lowers her gun.*

(to **SCUD***)* Now let your sergeant take the gun

> **SCUD** *is reluctant.*

ENYALIUS Sir I need to get you back inside

TALTHYBIA *(to* **SCUD***)* None of this is your responsibility

I can see that you are just a child

SCUD*, enraged by this, aims his gun at her again.*

SCUD I am not a child

I am a soldier

PHAEAX *fires.* **SCUD** *falls against* **TALTHYBIA***, shot.* **PLAUTUS** *is disarming* **MEGAERA***;* **ENYALIUS** *and* **ICHNAEA***;* **MILETUS***.* **MEGAERA** *is thrown to the ground,* **PLAUTUS**' *foot on her back.* **TALTHYBIA** *crying out in horror.*

MILETUS No, No –

MEGAERA SCUD

PLAUTUS / On your face

MEGAERA SCUD

PLAUTUS / I want you on your face

MILETUS NO

EURYDICE What have you done?

TALTHYBIA *cries out.*

ICHNAEA / It's OK

Talthybia it's cool

PARGEIA Get in there. Pick him up –

HAEMON *(to* **ISMENE***)* Take me to him

PARGEIA I said pick him up

TYDEUS *does so.*

THESEUS He was about to kill one of my staff

THALIA Oh Gods / Oh Gods

AGLAEA Disaster /

Disaster

TYDEUS I've got you soldier

THESEUS Who is in charge?

MILETUS I got him through the war

Right through the war

I saw him through it to the end

And now you cunts

PHAEAX We did our job

/ We did what's right

ENYALIUS / Shut up

MILETUS You've no idea

No fucking clue

PLUTUS Don't move

THESEUS Who controls this rabble?

EURYDICE I'm responsible

THESEUS Where is your Chief of Staff?

EURYDICE I haven't yet appointed one

TYDEUS It should be me, Prince Tydeus

AGLAEA Never

TYDEUS You can't have a military force without a leader

/ This is the result

EURYDICE I am the leader

Will you call your men away?

MILETUS Why aren't you trying to save him?

HAEMON I am trying

MILETUS You're a blind man

/ Gods

> **THESEUS** *gestures. His men lower their guns.* **SCUD** *is dying.*

HAEMON Who has first aid? One of you Athenians must have first
aid

PHAEAX I'm trained

I have first aid

HAEMON THEN MOVE

How can you watch me and not help?

HE'S DYING

PHAEAX and ICHNAEA go to assist.

MEGAERA SCUD

/ SCUD

TYDEUS Weak Theban leadership has almost killed King Theseus

EUPHROSYNE You damned hyena

Here to feast upon a dead boy's corpse

TYDEUS You almost sent the hope of Athens

Home to his good people in a box

/ This is how incapable these women are

THALIA Theseus, this is a war criminal

He means destruction / I can promise you

TYDEUS Who knows the situation with these armed militias? Me

Who can control them? Me

Who do you need here?

PARGEIA Prince Tydeus

HAEMON Get him in

ALL OF YOU GET HIM INSIDE

I need clean water

Bright dazzling lights

Ismene

ISMENE Here

HAEMON Help me

THALIA Take him in there. Get him on the table

They exit, **MILETUS, MEGAERA** *and* **THALIA** *with them.*

AGLAEA *(to* **EUPHROSYNE***)* We're going to the barracks, now.

We need the remnants of the army on our side

EUPHROSYNE / I am with you

They exit.

PARGEIA *(to* **TYDEUS***)* Go to your men; prepare them.

TYDEUS His blood is

PARGEIA Give me some

TYDEUS Piglets

PARGEIA I'll say I held him by your side

TYDEUS Mamma would never pay the butcher for the task;
We'd hang them up and slit their piggy throats.

PARGEIA Forget the pigs

TYDEUS Catching all the splatter in a pail

PARGEIA Tell Theseus you love him. Now

TYDEUS I am at your service, Theseus

All go except **EURYDICE,** **THESEUS** *and* **ANTIGONE.**

The bodyguards also remain; on high alert.

HARMONIA *has watched the death of* **SCUD** *with horror.*

She is riveted by all that follows.

EURYDICE You sanctioned murder in my house

THESEUS I think you'll find that I contained an incident

EURYDICE Who rules this land now Theseus?

THESEUS It's ruled by every wild-card with a gun who walks in
through your gates. My mandate's to / protect my people

EURYDICE Your mandate's to provide peacekeepers; not to start
another war

THESEUS Who was aggressor there?

EURYDICE The men who shot that boy

THESEUS They kept the peace

EURYDICE I had the peace. I had it in my hand. He was about to /
give away his gun

THESEUS To kill my citizen

ANTIGONE I'm fighting with the gods of death

They are above ground

I'm trying to appease

To do what they require

THESEUS She was burying her brother

Who would not?

ANTIGONE I've fought with them and begged

And now

They're feeding on that boy.

This is not

Is not my destiny

TALTHYBIA *enters. She is covered in blood.*

TALTHYBIA He's dead. Your son tried what he could but

EURYDICE Thank you very much, Talthybia

TALTHYBIA The table

He is lying on the table

Blood

The documents are

All his blood

TIRESIAS The sun will not race through the day

Before you have surrendered up

One born of your own loins

To feed the gods of death, for what you've done

THESEUS What is it with that hag?

EURYDICE Tiresias

THESEUS Why do you tolerate her here?

How can a modern state have room for this?

(to **TIRESIAS** *)* Who were you speaking to? To her
Or me? Whose loins?
What the fuck are loins supposed to be?
Do men and women both have loins –
Well do they?

TALTHYBIA I don't know sir

THESEUS What do you have, hag?

TIRESIAS The day comes soon when grief
Will break like waves through halls of power.
A suicide and then a son

THESEUS Whose son?

EURYDICE What suicide?

TIRESIAS It's coming. It will come

ANTIGONE Many years ago when Oedipus was young
Tiresias saved Thebes. There was an epidemic
And his revelations saved us. He said
My father was the curse upon our land.
Oedipus was murderous incestuous corruption
And his children, all of us so small
He called a crowd of horrors

EURYDICE Antigone

THESEUS What else has she foreseen?

EURYDICE I never listen to a word

THESEUS What has it said?

EURYDICE Tiresias has only ever spoken once to me. It was just
before you came I took it as a joke. He said

TIRESIAS 'If you intend to fuck the god of power, don't fall asleep
beside him'

THESEUS And do you?

EURYDICE Do I what?

THESEUS Intend to fuck with him

EURYDICE I don't see him anywhere

THESEUS Miss

TALTHYBIA My name's / Talthybia

THESEUS Could you please organise an imminent departure?

EURYDICE DON'T

THESEUS Since I stepped on Theban soil I've felt unclean; as if your vile, atavistic war was all my goddamn fault. / How dare you

EURYDICE Are we not behaving like the pets you hoped to tame?

Are you discovering instead of women pliable and biddable

That we're passionate and human; that we're free?

No one wants a strong and healthy Thebes, not you, not Sparta

THESEUS From now on you will be dealing with my people. My sense of international responsibility, my goddamn decency prevents me pulling out my men today

EURYDICE You're going to run away?

THESEUS My personal involvement with you ends right now

EURYDICE That is not leadership

THESEUS My life was put in danger here. I could have died

EURYDICE DON'T GO

THESEUS You have / not said a single word

EURYDICE Do not abandon us

THESEUS There has been no apology

EURYDICE I'm begging you

I'm sorry

Please don't go

THESEUS Pathetic

> **THESEUS** *exits.* **PHAEAX** *enters, also covered in blood. He is doing his best to clean his hands with surgical wipes.*

PHAEAX Where's Theseus? We need to know what his instructions are for the disposal of the body

EURYDICE THAT IS THEBAN BUSINESS

TALTHYBIA Theseus has just informed us that his diplomatic mission here is over

PHAEAX Oh

TALTHYBIA Have you got anything to say?

PHAEAX I have some wipes here

You should use them

You should really clean yourself

The blood you know

It might be

Look

I've only got first aid

I'm not a surgeon

And that Theban guy

He couldn't see

I saved your life

You were down there in the dust

That psycho had a gun right at your head

I was aiming for his arm, OK? *(he approaches her)*

You know I'm not at liberty to take responsibility for this

If I accept responsibility then our insurance policy won't cover me

There is a protocol I have to follow here, you know that.

But off the record, strictly off the record

Sorry

TALTHYBIA You are going to be my bitch

You understand that?

You are now my bitch

TALTHYBIA *exits.*

PHAEAX Fuck

PHAEAX *exits.* **HARMONIA** *inches forward.*

EURYDICE So this is not your destiny?

ANTIGONE *shakes her head.*

I can't believe

That you would side

With Prince Tydeus and the tyrant's wife

I thought that your integrity was absolute

So pure you make the rest of us feel tainted

ANTIGONE For me alone

I had to bury him

EURYDICE Why?

ANTIGONE Because it's right

EURYDICE Out of your rightness what will come?

A boy is dead

The citizen of Athens turns his back

I should throw you in a stinking cell for this

What do you think will happen?

ANTIGONE Send me to the dark

EURYDICE So Prince Tydeus can take up your part?

That widowed spider's spinning up support;

The forces I have tried so hard to quell

Are baying once again for power

This is the entry into chaos

ANTIGONE Let me

In the dark and squalor of a cell

Give me the means

I'll kill myself

To die is to be free

EURYDICE Antigone

ANTIGONE I'm no different from my brother

    I have a violent, prehistoric heart

    I should be dead with Polynices

    Let me be dead

EURYDICE I could have smothered him in flesh dissolving lime

    And dumped him in the ground

    But

    What he did to Creon, to Menoceus my boy –

    What he did to Thebes

    I hated him

    I hate him

    My heart is violent and it's vengeful too

    And I have dressed it up as reparation

    Shrouded it in reconciliation

    Saying maybe we will learn from staring at his face

    The face of chaos. Maybe we'll choose life,

    Life and order and society

    As the alternative is him. But when

    I stared down at the mottled thing

    I felt euphoria of savage hate

    It made me glad to see him rot.

    It is an act of hatred that I've done

    A desecration

    And I'm guilty

    And it is my fault

    I caused that child soldier's death

    And lost the help of Athens.

    This is the match that lights my own destruction

    Not to do what I've exhorted all my countrymen to do;

    Be reconciled.

    I cannot reconcile

I hate him, still I hate

He took my boy and mutilated him

And if I'm full of vicious, unforgiving hate

The moderate and principled

New President of Thebes

What future is there for us?

ANTIGONE Ismene thinks about the future all the time and Haemon too.

I've never understood their lack of fear.

My future's always been the desolate track

I walked on with my father

Leading on ahead past rotting crops and bloated dogs

Through burning villages, through war.

Oedipus was saved the sight

But I saw my destiny, my destination

Death

EURYDICE Oedipus

The way he fed upon your spirit

Took the youth in you and made it old

Dragged your hand through all his suffering

He was a selfish, blind old man.

HARMONIA *looks from* **ANTIGONE** *to* **TIRESIAS.** **TIRESIAS** *requires a drink. She serves him.*

My son Haemon is in love with you

I wish it was Ismene but it's you

You know that, don't you

ANTIGONE Yes

EURYDICE You see the antidote to suffering

The opposite of great heroic destiny

Is a quiet ordinary life; to love.

You've done enough for death, Antigone

You can retire from service I would say

Tiresias please tell her she is free

TIRESIAS I only see a suicide

A woman hanging by the neck

Her hair like trailing moss

EURYDICE You are despicable

TIRESIAS I wish I could see differently

The shadow of that boy

He's watching you

This deeply unsettles **HARMONIA**. *She backs away, distressed.*

ANTIGONE What's to be done?

EURYDICE There's no such thing as destiny

There's only change

ANTIGONE Please will you bury my brother?

EURYDICE You're asking me to admit my mistake

ANTIGONE You already have

EURYDICE In politics, I'll die

ANTIGONE I never see the politics

I'm blind to them

EURYDICE No, you see too clearly;

You've always seen through me

Right through my careful mask.

If I am weak

If I turn round and put that carcass in the earth

I fear the enemies of freedom

Will run me down like painted wolves

The soldiers, **HAEMON**, **ISMENE** *and the senators enter. They are carrying the dead* **JUNIOR LIEUTENANT**. **HARMONIA** *picks up* **TIRESIAS**'s *staff. She sings, high and free. A funeral song.*

HARMONIA The gods of death
Have feasted here

Lift your soul
Up to Elysium

May you be free
May you be free

EURYDICE *and* **ANTIGONE** *kneel down. The procession passes with* **HARMONIA** *a part of it. They exit after it.* **TIRESIAS** *remains.*

TYDEUS *and* **PARGEIA** *enter separately.* **TYDEUS** *has his bloodstained shirt in one hand.*

ACT FOUR

Digging

Two graves. The senators between them, **ANTIGONE, HAEMON, ISMENE, MILETUS, MEGAERA;** *bystanders,* **POLYKLEITOS** *among them.* **EURYDICE** *stares at both graves, covered with the mud of digging.*

HAEMON The crowd, Mumma

They need to hear you speak

EURYDICE *is silent, head bowed.*

Talk to the crowd

EURYDICE This heavy mask of power.

It will tear off my face

HAEMON When they pulled the shrapnel from my eyes.

And I was lying, knowing that my useful life was over

You washed me, dressed me and you said get up.

I'd have liked it if you'd rained down tears

But you handed me a stick. Get up

HAEMON *helps her up. She turns to the crowd.*

THALIA Your strongest words

EURYDICE By insulting Polynices

I've insulted all the dead.

I have been wrong

I'm trying to turn back time one hour

And it keeps buckling against me, flying on

The death of Junior Lieutenant Scud
Is my responsibility
I won't insult him with my sorrow and my shame
But I must give his death some value
Since his life was held so cheap.
Today, we've buried two dead Theban boys;
One, in life a mighty powerful man
One still a child, without a proper name.
General Polynices, son of Oedipus
And Junior Lieutenant Scud.
The way we treat these boys in death
Must illuminate how we intend to live
The Junior Lieutenant will be honoured,
Foremost son of Thebes.
Polynices will lie at his feet,
Marked only with his name.
In death, the general will wait upon the child

THALIA In death, the general will wait upon the child

POLYKLEITOS *kneels.* **THALIA** *kneels. The rest follow suit.*

Elsewhere: **TYDEUS** *and* **PARGEIA**.

TYDEUS My arteries are coursing with my god
My Dionysus, my amphetamine

PARGEIA Where are our men?

TYDEUS They're plucked up from the gutters, shacks and bars
Shaken, made alive with guns.
I've been up there on my truck
With Spartan weapons in my hand
Preaching revolution, Theban style.
The coup, swift and irrevocable
Has always favoured men like me –

PARGEIA Stop now

Hold back

You keep them on the leash

TYDEUS The open tear in time won't last

I feel it closing even now –

PARGEIA Eurydice has left the web.

The big presidential spider

Should be in the centre

Feeling every shift upon the net

But she's gone, she's scuttled off

Theseus is all alone up here

And enmity's between him and Eurydice

TYDEUS I have to do some politics

PARGEIA Shape up to it, come on, shape up

Shine up that skilful tongue of yours

We could have Theseus without the violence.

If Athens backs us Thebes is ours – elections all be fucked

You know it's Athens chooses leaders, props them up.

All this bla bla bla about democracy –

If they don't like the people's choice they topple it

TYDEUS Why do you always have the fucking plan?

He tries to kiss her.

PARGEIA No time for that

Not yet my Prince

But soon

She gives him a promise of something more.

Don't go in to Theseus all painted like a wolf

That gives the wrong impression straight away

TYDEUS I'm going for gold, Pargeia

PARGEIA Go for gold

BY THE GRAVES:

EUPHROSYNE *and* **AGLAEA** *speak intimately with* **EURYDICE**.

AGLAEA Tydeus has coiled up his men

And they are waiting

Stationed round the palace set to spring

EUPHROSYNE We have secured the military with promises of money we don't have. The remnants of the factions – they will fight for you

EURYDICE It must not come to that

Our mission must remain a peaceful one

Or what have we become?

EUPHROSYNE Our government's unique in all the world. It is worth fighting for

EURYDICE Our government will be unique if we can maintain power without resort to violence. That is the thing worth fighting for

AGLAEA I have imposed a no-fly zone

Under the circumstances it seemed pertinent.

It also means that Theseus can't leave

EURYDICE You genius

AGLAEA You must get back

To spend hours kneeling in the sun

It is not wise

EURYDICE It was essential

PARGEIA *enters.*

PARGEIA Thebes, you do not have a President, you have a coward

First she desecrates my husband's corpse

And then, when she perceives the horror of her crime

She quickly throws my Polynices in the ground

ANTIGONE Did your husband bury those he slew?

EURYDICE Antigone

ANTIGONE Their bodies rot there still in fields and streets.

And now he's dead you've got the next best thing

Apprentice tyrant Prince Tydeus

PARGEIA Tydeus is the leader that we need

He will keep order here in Thebes

ANTIGONE I saw his order in our villages

Women, little girls

All dead and stinking

Seething with the ants

MEGAERA *cocks her gun at* **ANTIGONE** – *an automatic gesture of defence. Silence falls.*

PARGEIA You have no shred of evidence against the Prince

ISMENE I do

MEGAERA *turns the gun on* **PARGEIA** – *then lowers it and stands with her.*

PARGEIA Thebans, Theseus is leaving

Eurydice has driven him away.

He is packing up

And with him goes our hope.

Who wants their children to be fed?

Who wants a future of prosperity?

March with me to the palace

Where your prince is now with Theseus

Prince Tydeus, trying to mend

What this incompetent has broken.

Democracy has never been the Theban way

We need a leader

It is he

The prince

Come with me for the prince

MEGAERA The prince

PARGEIA The prince

ERIS We must have order here

HELIA He will bring chaos

XENOPHANES He'll bring clarity

HELIA /Xenophanes, Bia

EUPHROSYNE /How can you betray us?

THALIA /Hold firm

Hold firm

AGLAEA Sisters

EURYDICE Remember where we came from

We would all lay down our lives for Thebes

Stand firm

PARGEIA exits. MEGAERA follows with some of the crowd. Cries of 'the prince'.

I wish that Thebes could mend itself without the rich world's help. I wish that we could find the unity, the strength. But in the meantime invite the Spartans to the talks

AGLAEA Thank you

I must confess

I did already

They arrive tonight

Say nothing; sack me later

EURYDICE You should be our leader

AGLAEA Yes but no one likes me. They elected you

EURYDICE Citizens of Thebes

Theseus is not about to leave

We will secure his friendship – that I promise you.

In less than one hour's time

We will have the hand of Athens in our own

And all our future hopes secure

She turns to go.

AGLAEA Can we deliver that?

EURYDICE Now I've said it, we will have to

EURYDICE *exits with her senators.*

THALIA You said 'I do'
Evidence
Tydeus
What do you have?

ISMENE Nothing
I have nothing, no

THALIA Please find your courage

ISMENE No evidence
I scrubbed it all away

THALIA Polykleitos
Speak
Please, while Theseus is here –

POLYKLEITOS I don't think I could get my mouth to move

THALIA What if the prince becomes respectable?
That's what he intends
Come with me

POLYKLEITOS Who'd believe? The people who can shout with passion always win. There is no point

HAEMON They win because the men like you, the best of us, keep quiet

THALIA *and* **POLYKLEITOS** *leave.*

ISMENE I'm leaving, going to Athens. I'll ask Theseus to let me tag along; a souvenir of Thebes. In Athens, I wouldn't have to be a relic from this house. I could wear jeans and smoke

ANTIGONE How can you be flippant?

ISMENE I think it's in my nature, buried under years, to be quite shallow and to laugh. I think alone of Oedipus' children I've got a sense of humour. Burying our brother nearly split my sides. And the biggest joke of all is that Haemon has proposed. He has asked you, Antigone, to be his wife.

It was a nice proposal; very sweet.

But by mistake

The stupid, eyeless oaf made it to me.

(to **HAEMON***)* I've been in love with you since I was nine

ISMENE *exits.*

ANTIGONE Ismene

ISMENE

ANTIGONE *runs off after her.*

MILETUS You failed that boy

HAEMON I'm blind

MILETUS I should blow those empty sockets through your skull

HAEMON I'm sorry that I couldn't save him

MILETUS Early in the war, the general I was with would kill a child before each fight and we would drink the blood. The place I was, was so far gone

That I could see no harm. One night I woke to find a bushknife at my neck, a woman holding it. Her hands were stinking with our blood. I was the only soldier she had left alive.

'You are our sons,' she said

And in me what was human woke. She said she'd spare my life and lift her curse if I could save as many as I'd killed. I managed only two

Just one remains

HARMONIA *sings.* **MILETUS** *leaves his gun on* **SCUD** *'s grave. He exits.*

HARMONIA *gives* **HAEMON TIRESIAS** *' staff. She exits.*
ANTIGONE *enters.*

ANTIGONE Ismene said "Can you not see?"

HAEMON Antigone

ANTIGONE I want to see
    What life is like
    To live

ACT FIVE

Scene One
Storytelling

THESEUS *and* **TYDEUS** *enter.*

TYDEUS The women turn him on
They get him all worked up with dancing
Then they run off to the mountains
To perform their rites.
And Pentheus can't find
The thing, you know
The thing that makes us men

TALTHYBIA *enters.*

THESEUS He loses his

TYDEUS Not physically –
All the inside stuff

THESEUS Testosterone?

TYDEUS Not quite

TALTHYBIA Excuse me, Theseus
This is Prince Tydeus

THESEUS Yes, I know that

TALTHYBIA He's accused of war crimes

THESEUS I think I left the phone you gave me in my quarters.
Would you go and see if there's a message from my son?

TALTHYBIA *exits.*

So Pentheus is unmanned

TYDEUS With the help of Dionysus he applies some makeup and
he dresses up

THESEUS He wants to find out what it's like to be a woman?

TYDEUS Have you never wondered, sir?

The myths are where we risk

What we would never think in life.

Pentheus was mad with longing

He was desperate to join the rites

THESEUS To dance

TYDEUS He follows them into the wild

He climbs a tree

He watches all their secrets

Feels as isolated as a star

He cries

His tears go splash upon the women underneath

They look up.

Red alert

A man in drag

THESEUS What do they do?

TYDEUS I can't believe you come to Thebes and you don't know
this story. That great gang of naked women dragged Pentheus
on to the ground and pulled him limb from limb with their
bare hands. Those ladies and those little girls dismembered
him. They tore his dick off and his head off and his own
mother and his aunts were playing with his body parts like they
were bits of ram goat ready for the grill

THESEUS Shit

The sound of a crowd begins to approach.

TYDEUS That's quite a story isn't it?

THESEUS That's fucking elemental

TYDEUS It's true

(pointing to **TIRESIAS**) She was there

TIRESIAS The furies

Zeus himself bows down to them

One of them is coming

An avenger to destroy you

THESEUS Oh shut up

Shut up

I'm going to build a care home here

For beggarly transgender types

I'm going to take you off the street

Stick you on a rocking chair in front of a TV

And feed you the strongest psychotropic drugs

That medicine can buy

TIRESIAS Where is my child?

I bought her from her mother

She is mine

TYDEUS You can see why we're all wary of the womenfolk round here

PHAEAX *enters.*

PHAEAX Sir, we've just been told that Thebes is in a state of high alert. Crowds are marching through the streets. A no-fly zone has been imposed

THESEUS Excuse me?

PHAEAX Air space has been / prohibited

THESEUS I know what a no-fly zone is

PHAEAX The Theban senators insist we stay in our chambers until such time as they can guarantee our safety

THESEUS Are you a moron?

PHAEAX No sir

THESEUS Yes, I think you are

PHAEAX This information you may judge to be moronic. I am merely its deliverer

THESEUS You pulled your trigger on that boy. You were his deliverer. It was moronic

TALTHYBIA *enters.*

PHAEAX We were aiming to disarm, not kill.

We followed your own protocol

I protected you

And then I tried to save his life.

I don't know why I'm getting all this shit

TALTHYBIA *(handing* **THESEUS** *the mobile)* Theseus, you have no messages

THESEUS *hands the mobile to* **PHAEAX**.

THESEUS Get me my son, Hippolytus. I want to talk to him right now. He's stationed up at Troezen under General Pirithous. Young man

PHAEAX Yes sir

THESEUS Don't cry in front of me

PHAEAX *exits.*

Tell Eurydice that I have no intention of resuming talks

TALTHYBIA Sir, if I may –

THESEUS Her no-fly zone is a pathetic ruse to keep me here

TALTHYBIA There's a crowd approaching, some / sort of protest –

THESEUS Get it lifted, crowd or not

TALTHYBIA *exits.*

Those women ripping up King Pentheus;

That's just a myth; that's not your history, right?

TYDEUS All violence in Thebes is mythic

It soon fades into the past

Loses its immediacy and force.

You'll find our civil war is mythic too

Blown into distorted shapes.

The violence happened

But it wasn't real

THESEUS That's a disturbing answer

TYDEUS I can keep order here in Thebes

I'd see your will was done.

I'd make sure that Thebes becomes whatever you desire

Thebes needs a man like you;

You're strong and clear; you give us hope

And in this small, material world

First citizen of Athens

You're the nearest thing to Dionysus that I've ever seen

PHAEAX *enters. The sound of the crowd is much nearer.*

PHAEAX Sir, I spoke with General Pirithous. He says your son Hippolytus is absent without leave. He left the base last night to see your wife, at your request. Since then, nothing has been heard of him. The general is offering to search your coastal residence

THESEUS Thank him. Tell him yes

PHAEAX There is a crowd sir, gathering down there. The peacekeepers await your orders. What should I be telling them?

THESEUS To keep the peace

PHAEAX And how should they interpret that?

THESEUS Could you get out of here?

PHAEAX *exits.*

I'm strangely

Since I got here I have –

My conviction, yes, my certainty has gone.

My easy access to the gods themselves;

Suddenly it's all obscured.

I feel some revelation, some disaster is at hand

TYDEUS Theseus

THESEUS Said way too much. I'm going to walk away

TYDEUS It's Thebes that is off-centre, not yourself.

You stick an upright man into a gale,

A cyclone, and the cyclone will prevail.

Thebes hasn't done with chaos yet.

PARGEIA enters. MEGAERA *stays by the door. She watches* PRINCE
TYDEUS *closely.*

Eurydice will never hold it back

The very female nature is chaotic.

They can't structure or impose

They won't inspire respect

The woman

She should do what she was made for

PARGEIA And what's that?

TYDEUS Pargeia

PARGEIA I've led the people up to greet you, Theseus

They would so appreciate a glimpse

Some kind of indication that you care.

Shall we go out before the people?

THESEUS For what?

PARGEIA News has been leaked that you are going to leave us.
Violence is erupting. People feel Eurydice has let them down;
they feel betrayed. They've come to beg you not to go. I know
you haven't taken well to Thebes but we could find a lot of
ways to make your visits here a pleasure

EURYDICE enters with AGLAEA *and* EUPHROSYNE. *She is still
covered in dirt from digging.*

EURYDICE Theseus

You are free to leave at any time.

We will ensure safe passage through our airspace

THESEUS Have you still got authority?

EURYDICE Thank you for everything you've done here

It has been a pleasure speaking with you – genuinely.

Now if you'll excuse us, we've a conference to prepare

We expect the Spartans shortly

THESEUS What?

EUPHROSYNE The Spartans are arriving

EURYDICE I was hoping beggars could be choosers but it seems we can't

THESEUS Let me tell you about Sparta

EUPHROSYNE We are not ignorant

THESEUS The Spartans do not tolerate the weak

AGLAEA We are not weak

THESEUS They feel no responsibility to improve your lot. They're here to feast upon your natural resources. You can be sure of that

AGLAEA And Athens offers us an economic zone

THESEUS They'll strip you bare

EURYDICE Our people go to bed with hunger craving in their bellies every night. Right now we'll entertain any regime that gives us means to feed them

THESEUS If you want an independent, democratic Thebes –

EURYDICE Mine are the politics of dire need.

I am president of famine

First citizen of rubble, plague and debt

And hungry dogs are scavenging the waste

Athens, Sparta

If you cannot help

May you devour yourselves

THESEUS I can't believe you'd speak to me like this.

I came here so compassionate

So full of energy, of admiration;

I was going to pledge myself to your improvement.

You make me feel like I'm a wicked man

And I don't like that, not one bit.

I AM THE HOPE OF ATHENS AND THE WORLD

EURYDICE Then come out with me and tell the crowd.

Pause.

TYDEUS How can I assist you Theseus

Because to bring the Spartans into things

That is an insult

I'm insulted here on your behalf

PARGEIA After everything you've done for Thebes

TYDEUS I would never deal with the Spartans

EUPHROSYNE Unless you're buying weapons from them

TYDEUS You know what I'm reminded of?

With all these ladies situated here

Hyenas trying their weight against the lions

TALTHYBIA *enters with* **THALIA** *and* **POLYKLEITOS**.

THESEUS Tabitha, I asked my aide to make a call for me –

TALTHYBIA My name's Talthybia

Please have the courtesy to get it right.

This is Polykleitos, a mechanic

And you know the minister of justice, Thalia

THALIA Please will you witness this man's testimony?

POLYKLEITOS You were my hero

I taught my son to love you

We had you on a poster

Your face

Tacked up on our garage wall.

I've meditated on your face

That tsetse face

TYDEUS I don't know you, brother

POLYKLEITOS We were hiding from the massacre

My son was terrified.

His name was Opheltes and he was five years old

You shot the locks

We saw you kick the door

The light surrounded you

That grin.

My son, he ran to you

As if you were a hero come to save us.

And

You pinned him on a bayonet

You lifted him

Laughed at your strength as you held him aloft

Shaking the gun

The blood dropped like rain

My boy

Bewildered at his death.

Your twisting laugh;

It rings in my ears in the night

TYDEUS I don't know you

POLYKLEITOS You killed my son

You burned my home

You don't know me

I am the coward who hid

And watched the flames

Even as they

Even as they ate

TYDEUS I'm so sorry for your loss

But you're mistaken, friend

POLYKLEITOS I know the moment lies in wait for you

When Opheltes in all his blood-dimmed innocence

Will step into your mind and shake your sanity to pieces

MEGAERA Woosh

POLYKLEITOS I'd like to go

> **POLYKLEITOS** *exits with* **THALIA**. *The noise of the restless crowd is louder.*

EURYDICE Excuse me

The future will not wait

AGLAEA Thank you for your interest in Thebes

PARGEIA Theseus, if you would step outside with Prince Tydeus and myself, I think that we could calm the situation down

THESEUS You must be so naive

Political babies, both of you.

You are untouchable;

A tyrant's wife, a warlord

TYDEUS But privately, when you and I were speaking

THESEUS I don't recall I ever met you

This private conversation is a myth

TYDEUS Our paths will cross again

Much sooner than you think

And when they do

We will remember this

> **TYDEUS** *and* **PARGEIA** *leave.* **MEGAERA** *follows them.*

THESEUS I'm cold

I felt a sudden fear go down my back

My hairs are standing up

TALTHYBIA Thebes has a very strong effect.

I'd like to stay here

I think we Athenians should stay

PHAEAX *enters.*

PHAEAX Sir, I've General Pirithous on the phone

THESEUS What is it?

PHAEAX He

Is at your home

THESEUS What is it?

Scene Two
Avenging

PARGEIA, TYDEUS, MEGAERA *enter.*

PARGEIA You fucked it up

    You fucked it up

TYDEUS You fat degenerate obscene salacious slut

PARGEIA I am not fat

TYDEUS You fucking threw yourself at him

PARGEIA You were in love with him

    I saw it in your eyes

    Big Theseus

    You dumb cocksucker

TYDEUS I had him so he almost called me brother

PARGEIA You would have given him your naked butt

    If I had not arrived.

    You're all the same, you men

    You go round raping women to disguise the fact

    You like it from each other best

TYDEUS You're filth

PARGEIA I'm debris, I am waste, I'm dereliction, I am frenzy

TYDEUS You could survive in hell itself

PARGEIA I have

    Give your men the word

TYDEUS It's time

PARGEIA Unleash the god of uproar on this town

TYDEUS Uproar

PARGEIA Cry fury

TYDEUS / Fury

MEGAERA Fury

> **MEGAERA** *stabs* **TYDEUS**.

PARGEIA Prince

MEGAERA For my sisters and my mother
> For the village by a river where I used to be a girl
> Let me go now furies
> Let me go

> **MEGAERA** *exits*.

Scene Three
Cursing

EURYDICE *is washing.* **ISMENE** *waiting.*

EURYDICE I can go out without him
Go out before the people quite alone
I'll tell them Thebes must find a way
To be a nation that regenerates itself
That without the crumbs of help
From monstrous foreign powers
We can begin to grow

ISMENE That is a fantasy
I'm sorry but your optimism's ludicrous
It sickens me

EURYDICE Ismene

ISMENE What special quality allows you to believe
That you can challenge or change anything?

EURYDICE What's happened?
My sweet girl

ISMENE Not sweet
Not girl
Forgive me
I have not survived this war

THESEUS *enters.*

THESEUS You refuse to see me

EURYDICE This is my private room

THESEUS That is childish

And it is a great mistake

EURYDICE I have not refused to see you I am washing

THESEUS I offered you equality

EURYDICE No you did not

THESEUS It's not equality you want

You think yourself superior in every way

Behaving like a prehistoric queen

EURYDICE Theseus, I am a beggar not a queen

I beg you to keep faith with me

And with my government.

Come before the people with me please

Or everything I'm fighting for is lost.

I have no desire to sell myself to Sparta

If it comes to that then I would rather dance for you

Pause.

THESEUS Two snakes, slithering mistrust

That's what your prophet said.

Do you think in essence

That it's like that with a woman and a man?

EURYDICE If they're politicians.

I would love to trust you, Theseus

THESEUS I got a call

From General Pirithous

He is in my house

He said

EURYDICE What is it?

THESEUS Phaedra

She is dead

THESEUS *is suddenly exhausted, as if a great shock has hit him.*

EURYDICE Ismene

    ISMENE *gets a stool.*

THESEUS Phaedra
    She is hanging
    Hanging from the beam
    Above our bed

    THESEUS *half collapses. She helps him on to the stool.*

    The scale of chaos here;
    To mend it is beyond me.
    The haemorrhage of cash
    The manpower it would need
    To bring Thebes to prosperity –

EURYDICE Theseus

I knew

That something in my life was going to break

Phaedra

My son

EURYDICE Where is he?

THESEUS They don't know

What did he do to her?

He hated her

EURYDICE You cannot know that it was him

THESEUS Curse him

EURYDICE Please don't say that

THESEUS Curse him

EURYDICE You are speaking in your grief

THESEUS I know your government is brave

And you deserve success.

Forgive me but –

I haven't got the –

Cannot deal with Sparta

I'll come outside with you

Give you my hand

EURYDICE These fists of yours

One force, one gentleness

Open them

THESEUS How could she do that to herself?

EURYDICE The young feel such despair

THESEUS Athens

Come to Athens

We will reconvene

You have my word

EURYDICE Athens

THESEUS For Thebes to thrive –

EURYDICE We must believe that it's possible

That we can change

We have to risk our trust

They exit, out to the crowd.

Elsewhere:

Aides prepare for a departure taking all the paraphernalia of a diplomatic visit.

POLYKLEITOS *continues his work.*

The senators enter, preparing for the arrival of the Spartans.

Through the politics, **ANTIGONE**, *leading the blind men.*

ISMENE, *dressed in Athenian clothes, pleads with* **PHAEAX** *to be let on the helicopter. He is unforthcoming. She exits after him, still pleading.*

TALTHYBIA *enters.* **TIRESIAS**' *child is holding papers for her. They crouch together in the blast.* **TALTHYBIA** *loses her hairdo. They exit, as the noise of the helicopter begins to fade.*

TIRESIAS Numberless indignant birds

Are making storm clouds in Athenian skies.

Greed that eats, will eat itself.

Athens' time will come

EPILOGUE

Walking

Dust and emptiness – but for the figure of **MILETUS**. **MEGAERA** *enters.*

MEGAERA Miletus, where are you going?

MILETUS Athens

MEGAERA Why?

MILETUS Because I want

MEGAERA Want what?

MILETUS That stuff they got

MEGAERA And what's that?

MILETUS Everything

MEGAERA But Athens

They won't let us in

MILETUS You coming too?

MEGAERA I'll keep you company

As long as you don't give me all your shit

MILETUS Be fair

MEGAERA That sergeant shit

Don't try and pull that

You are not my sergeant now

MILETUS I'm just the man that's standing here

His pockets full of breeze.

There's nothing more to me than this

MEGAERA That's man enough for me

MILETUS Glad to hear it

Glad you finally have eyes

MEGAERA So how you going to get to Athens, in your limousine?

MILETUS The Theban way

MEGAERA How's that?

MILETUS On my big Theban feet

MEGAERA It's far away

MILETUS So far away they got a different sky

MEGAERA They don't like Thebans there

MILETUS Athens has a lot of crime

MEGAERA That's right. It's quite a violent place

MILETUS You think you'll handle it?

MEGAERA I cannot wait. You think they'll stop us at the gates?

MILETUS Megaera, woman, what do you suggest?

MEGAERA Miletus, man,

They give us any shit

They stand there in their marble palaces and try to keep us out

We'll soak our rags in petrol

And we'll burn their city down.

Prologue

Property List

Megaera – Gun (p3)

Corpse (p4)

Scud – Rifle (p5)

Lighting

It is dawn (p1)

Act One

Property List

Pile of rifle parts (p6)

Talthybia – Bottled water, paperwork, bad choice of footwear (p6)

Other Athenian men and women enter in silk and linen suits; Theban officials in cheaper suits or trying to hold together their national dress in the face of the helicopter's gale (p7)

Bodyguards and aides cross with all the luggage and paraphernalia of a diplomatic story (p7)

Mobile phone (p8)

Polynices's corpse (p17)

Money (p21)

Document (p26)

Sound Effects

The sound of a helicopter approaching from afar (p6)

The helicopter, louder (p7)

A makeshift Theban choir begins to sing a national anthem (p7)

Force of the helicopter's gale (p7)

The helicopter becomes deafening (p7)

Everyone crouches in the blast (p7)

The blast dies down (p7)

Haemon's eyes have suffered serious injury (p21)

Act Two
Property List

As they speak the stage is being prepared for the inauguration (p29)

Podium (p31)

Cheque (p40)

Gun (p50)

Mobile phone (p50)

Clockwork radio (p55)

She picks up a handful of dust. She lets it fall through her fingers over the corpse. She repeats the gesture (p59)

Gun (p59)

Lighting

First light (p59)

Sound Effects

A rousing national anthem (p31)

Music (p55)

Act Three

Property List

Ismene is making coffee – a ceremony over charcoal (p60)

Coin (p60)

Surgical wipes (p78)

Tydeus – bloodstained shirt (p84)

Two graves (p85)

Mobile (p97)

Knife (p106)

Eurydice is washing (p107)

Stool (p109)

Aides prepare for a departure taking all the paraphernalia of a diplomatic visit (p110)

Ismene – dressed in Athenian clothes (p110)

Tiresias' child is holding papers for her (p111)

Sound Effects

Talthybia – covered in blood (p76)

Phaeax – also covered in blood (p78)

Eurydice – covered by the mud of digging (p85)

The sound of a crowd begins to approach (p95)

The sound of the crowd is much nearer (p98)

They crouch together in the blast....as the noise of the helicopter begins to fade (p111)

Epilogue
Sound Effects

Dust and emptiness (p112)

Lightning Source UK Ltd.
Milton Keynes UK
UKOW06f1623080416

271882UK00001B/3/P